641.373
Cil

161120

Davidson

P9-CAM-084

13,46

Making Great
CHEESE
At Home

DISCARD

161120

LARK BOOKS

A Division of Sterling Publishing Co., Inc.
New York

Making Great
CHEESE
At Home

30 SIMPLE RECIPES
FROM CHEDDAR TO CHÈVRE

PLUS 18
DELICIOUS
CHEESE DISHES

**Barbara
Ciletti**

Shelbyville-Shelby County
Public Library

BOBBE NEEDHAM
Editor

CHRIS BRYANT
Book and cover design and
production, food testing and
food styling, and photostyling

EVAN BRACKEN
Photography

HEATHER SMITH
Editorial assistance

HANNES CHAREN
Production assistance

VAL ANDERSON
Proofreader

Library of Congress Cataloging-in-Publication Data

Available

Ciletti, Barbara J.

    Making great cheese at home : 30 simple recipes from cheddar to chèvre plus 18 delicious cheese dishes / Barbara Ciletti.

10 9 8 7 6 5 4 3 2 1

Published by Lark Books, a division of
Sterling Publishing Co., Inc.
387 Park Avenue South, New York, N.Y. 10016

© 1999, Barbara Ciletti

Distributed in Canada by Sterling Publishing,
c/o Canadian Manda Group, One Atlantic Ave., Suite 105
Toronto, Ontario, Canada M6K 3E7

Distributed in Australia by Capricorn Link (Australia) Pty Ltd., P.O.
P.O. Box 704, Windsor, NSW 2756 Australia

Distributed in the U.K. by:
Guild of Master Craftsman Publications Ltd.
Castle Place 166 High Street, Lewes, East Sussex, England, BN7 1XU
Tel: (+ 44) 1273 477374 Fax: (+ 44) 1273 478606
Email: pubs@thegmcgroup.com Web: www.gmcpublications.com

The written instructions, photographs, designs, patterns, and projects in
this volume are intended for the personal use of the reader and may be
reproduced for that purpose only. Any other use, especially commercial
use, is forbidden under law without written permission of the copyright
holder.

Every effort has been made to ensure that all the information in this book
is accurate. However, due to differing conditions, tools, and individual
skills, the publisher cannot be responsible for any injuries, losses, and
other damages that may result from the use of the information in this
book.

If you have questions or comments about this book, please contact:
Lark Books
50 College St.
Asheville, NC 28801
(828) 253-0467
Printed in China

All rights reserved

ISBN 1-57990-267-7

acknowledgments

THIS BOOK brought together old friends and added a few new ones. I am really pleased for the opportunity to work with the abundant talents that come from the folks at Lark Books. Many thanks to my publisher, Carol Taylor, for inspiration and camaraderie throughout this bookmaking journey. Of course, such a journey gained momentum and beauty through the artistry of my art director, Chris Bryant, and the keen eye of photographer Evan Bracken. They make one terrific team. This book gained life through the guidance of my editor, Bobbe Needham; her skill and infectious good humor encouraged a volume that we can all be proud of. Thanks, Bobbe. You're the best.

Dialogue with a few knowledgeable pros clarified a number of the technicalities about making cheese. First and foremost, thanks to Jim Mildbrand of Wisby North America, for simplifying the complexities of cheese science. More information, recipes, and stories were shared by many. Thanks to Polly Fafach at Lakehaven Farms, who gave me a recipe along with cultural background for Finnish Leipäjuusto. Many thanks as well to Jane North at Northland Dairy, Paula Lambert at the Fresh Mozzarella Factory, Jonathan White and Warren Reed at Egg Farm Dairy, the American Cheese Society, Longmont Dairy, and Stephano Sarti and his crew at Il Forteto in Tuscany. These folks live their craft and share it joyfully.

contents

8 **Introduction**

10 **A Brief History of Cheese**

18 **The Craft of Making Great Cheese at Home**

32 **Thirty Great Cheeses to Make at Home**

Fresh, Soft,
and Semisoft
Cheeses

36 Fromage Blanc
38 Chèvre
40 Mascarpone
42 Herb Garden Cheese
45 Finnish Leipäjuusto
47 Cream Cheese
49 Cottage Cheese
52 Queso Blanco
54 Whole-Cream Ricotta
56 Whey Ricotta
57 Mozzarella
60 Stuffed Mozzarella
62 Braided Mozzarella
64 Scamorze
65 Weinkase

Mold- and
Age-Ripened
Cheeses

68 Stilton
71 All-American Brick
74 Danish Blue
77 Camembert

Age-Ripened
Hard Cheeses

80 Muenster
82 Feta
84 White Goat Cheddar
87 Yellow Aged Cheddar
90 Sage Cheddar
91 Holland Gouda
94 Romano
97 Parmesan
100 Raclette
103 Baby Swiss
106 Gjetost

108 Recipes for Extravagant Cheese Fare

Appetizers 109 Serenely Swiss Fondue
110 Danish Sesame Twists
111 Camembert Phyllo
112 Stilton Spring Salad
114 Gorgonzola Mascarpone Torte
116 Three-Cheese Herb Torte
117 Swiss Onion Flatbread
118 Lemon Mozzarella
with Parmesan Crostini

Main Dishes 120 Feta Spinach Olive Pie
& Breads 122 Gjetost Pizza
123 Chèvre Dill Muffins
124 Queso Blanco Enchiladas
126 Harvest Cheddar Poppy Bread
127 Ravioli Toscano

Desserts 130 Ricotta Pie
132 Tiramisu Tango
133 Fromage Strawberry Wreath
134 Gouda Apple Cobbler

136 Cheese-Makers' Sources

137 Metric Equivalents

138 Glossary

141 Bibliography

143 Index

introduction

MANY OF US WANT—even yearn—to make our own cheese at home. Much like people who prefer home-grown vegetables above all others, we are more than willing to trade the uniformity of store-bought cheese for the tactile pleasures, exciting tastes, and satisfying experience of making our own rounds of Cheddar, Gouda, or Parmesan. (We might as well get to the business of how to pronounce Gouda right now. The Dutch, from whom it hails, pronounce it how'da, a helpful tip if you're in the Netherlands and want to sound educated. But in North America and else-where, the pronunciation is goo'da.)

Regardless of the technology that allows people to enjoy cheese every day throughout the world, cheese making continues to be an art and a craft. Artisan groups in North America, as well as in Europe, South America, and Mexico, appreciate the rich tradition of cheese making and the rewards of making cheese by hand. In North America, for example, artisans regularly share their passions for cheese and dairy products at American Cheese Society gatherings.

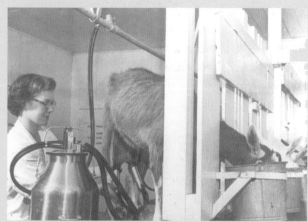

Helga Sandburg. Photograph courtesy of Paula Steichen.

Making cheese, like making our own wine, bread, and other foods that require controlled fermentation, can be a bit unwieldy until practice leads to skill. Time, temperature, live cultures, and patience become our teachers. This craft, like so many others, provides the opportunity for a little meditation, for putting a little more balance in your life. As you wait for the milk to warm or the curds to form and set, you can allow yourself to focus on the process and relax. As you engage in the pleasure of working with your hands, you can give your spirit a bit of breathing room.

I hope you'll have fun with the section in this book on history and cheese lore, then go on to the chapter on the craft—I've tried to make it a practical and approachable guide for making great cheese at home. You'll find explanations of the basic steps in the cheese-making process and of equipment and ingredients. The recipes for making thirty cheeses follow; you'll find old acquaintances, such as chèvre, mozzarella, Muenster, and brick, as well as more exotic varieties, including Danish blue and scamorze.

In the next section I've included a few of my favorite recipes for dishes that feature cheese, from appetizers to desserts. At the end of the book, you'll find a guide to sources for cheese-making supplies and tools and a glossary in which I've defined all the terms that may be unfamiliar to you.

Beyond the enjoyment of the flavors and natural ingredients of homemade cheese, I find that part of the pleasure of making it in my kitchen lies in the joy of sharing the cheese with my family and friends. Satisfaction in the process, pleasure in the eating, and joy in the sharing—I hope you'll find these, as I have. Enjoy!

a brief history of cheese

GO TO ALMOST ANY COUNTRY IN THE WORLD, and you will find cheese on the table, or in the refrigerator, or quietly aging to perfection. Its flavor, its aroma, its adaptability, and its nourishing goodness have made cheese a staple in homes and restaurants from Acapulco to Bern, Montpelier to Seattle. No matter the recipe or the menu, cheese is a staple in any language. A hearty and delicious food, it is also a sensual delight.

Draining cheese in an early Wisconsin cheese factory.
Photograph courtesy of State Historical Society of Wisconsin.

Discovering Cheese

As you would guess if you thought about it (and maybe you have), cheese appeared on the scene only after humans learned to domesticate animals. This happened during the Mesolithic age, as the blanket of ice that gripped large portions of the earth's surface began to recede from the areas we today know as central and southern Europe.

As the climate grew warmer, humans began to move around more freely and to hone their skills as hunters and gatherers. At least 8,000 years before the birth of Christ, especially in Persia and other parts of what we today call the Near East, they tamed the dog (which assisted in hunting), expanded their efforts to plant and harvest food, and began not only to keep but to herd and to propagate sheep and goats.

Somewhere along the line, some alert human discovered, perhaps by leaving a bowl of milk near a fire, that heat could curdle milk into a delicious and healthy mass of curds. According to archaeological finds, cheese was not only made, but molded and drained, as early as 2,700–2,800 B.C. We know that certain terra-cotta urns and bowls were made with cheese in mind, because before firing they were perforated with tiny holes for draining. And if the reed mats we use for air drying cheese today could speak, they would tell of their ancient cousins, which came together as so many meshed rushes taken from the river to the kitchen. Milk, whey, and human cheese lovers had formed a bond that lasts to this day.

Cheese Goes West

Until 350 B.C., cheese making probably remained a relatively small-scale industry. However, as humans extended their dominance over the land and animals, people dwelling in what is now central Europe began to domesticate cattle.

In the East, in spite of buffalo herds thoughout Asia, milk was less plentiful. In east Asia, down through most of history, herders and farmers have used milk primarily to suckle newborn calves and goats rather than collecting it for the kitchen.

In the West and in southwest Asia, fertile climates encouraged cows to give much greater quantities of milk than did ewes and goats. The plains along the Danube and other rivers offered the perfect diet for foraging bovines. Cows at that time probably produced three to four gallons daily per animal, about two and a half times sheep or goat production. Soon, not only were cheese makers turning out a ready source of nutrition, but cheese making had become a necessity, as shepherds and farmers found themselves with a surplus of milk. The goats and ewes that had provided the wherewithal for cheese making from the scrubby, rocky slopes of ancient Sumer, in Babylonia and Greece, had passed their legacy to larger animals in more verdant pastures.

The fertile land along the Tigris and Euphrates Rivers fed livestock, and especially cows, whose milk their owners transformed into a number of cheeses, butter, and other dairy products. Among them were cheeses flavored with honey, spices, fruits, and herbs, as creative cheese makers combined the various bounties of the Earth. The resident Sumerians, Hebrews, and Egyptians delighted in preparing feasts that celebrated their herd animals, and in spinning stories that transformed goats into gods.

No wonder ancient mythology includes tales of gods suckled by sheep and goats. These animals represented not just a source of physical strength and virility but the life force itself. Warriors carried cheese into battle, for it was a very practical food—it didn't need to be cooked, it contained plenty of protein and fat, and it was portable. It's not hard to imagine a biblical David with a bag of dried curds hanging from his belt. As the Bible story relates, he was delivering cheese and drink to his brothers in the field when he first encountered the giant Goliath.

When in Ancient Rome

Over the next few centuries, milk and cheese consumption continued to spread across the known world. The ancient Romans ate cheese every day, and by bathing in milk celebrated its role in preserving youth and vigor. As cheese makers came to better understand the process of making cheese, they requested that milking occur at dusk, when the sun's rays were less strong and thus less likely to spoil the milk. Although they put a good portion of the shepherds' bounty to immediate use, they learned to leave some milk in its gathering pot, lightly salted, for storage during the cooler winter months.

The great Roman philosopher Pliny the Elder raised cheese to new heights when he extolled its virtues in his *Natural History* in A.D. 77. His remarks about the Italian peninsula as a whole depicted people who delighted in making and consuming sheep's milk cheese from an area in northwest Italy, Liguria, as well as smoked goat's cheese, a favorite at the Roman markets.

The name *Parmesan* traces back to Old Italian's *parmigiano*—loosely translated, it means "in true Parma style," or "in the Parma tradition." Many centuries ago, this cheese was known for its heartiness and its grainy, chewy interior. Roman soldiers carried great wedges of Parmesan and pecorino, sturdy cheeses easy to cart around the countryside. These dryer, hard cheeses were less apt to spoil under the hot sun and staved off hunger during months of travel. (The name *pecorino* comes from *pecus*, the Latin word for domestic animals, via *pecora* and then *pecorino*, Italian for *sheep* and things *of sheep*. Thus it refers to any of a variety of Italian cheese made from sheep's milk.)

Setting the Dairy Industry Back

Who can resist a company whose motto is "Setting the dairy industry back 100 years"? The cheese industry's answer to Ben and Jerry's began in Jonathan White's kitchen. There he cooked and developed curds and meanwhile converted his basement into a curing room. In 1993 he teamed up with Charlie Palmer (owner/chef of New York City's Aureole restaurant) to found Egg Farm Dairy in Peekskill, New York.

EFD's first-class recipes for naturally ripened cheeses include Impe Dunder, a small round of ripened rind cheese, which carries its legend on its label: Apparently the early Dutch sailors who explored the Hudson River Highlands blamed their riparian misfortunes on a mischievous spirit that haunted the river at Dunder. As they sailed past Jan Peek's Kill (a kill is a creek or channel), they would tip their hats out of respect for Impe Dunder.

Bringing back the good old days: Jonathan White of Egg Farm Dairy. Photograph courtesy of Jonathan White.

Already famous for their "Wild-Ripened Cheeses"—handmade artisan cheeses that reflect "a uniquely American combination of agricultural fecundity and ethnic diversity"—the partners' goal may be within their reach: "to return butter and cheese to their lost grandeur."

Il Forteto

Making ricotta in Italy today—rinsing and draining ricotta curds at Il Forteta. Photograph by Eric Schreiber.

About twenty years ago, Stephano Sarti and a group of his fellow recent college graduates reclaimed an abandoned farm in Vicchio, in the rolling Tuscan hills about fifteen miles from Florence. They intended to build a cooperative community that could encourage a return to the artisan craft of cheese making. They wanted to create their own neighborhood, make cheese, rejuvenate the orchards, and cultivate the fields.

Today their Vicchio facility, Il Forteto (loosely translated: "strength from unity"), produces a cheese prized throughout Italy—Pecorino Toscano, a composite of sheep's milk, tradition, excruciatingly high standards of performance, and, of course, time. My husband, Eric, and I visited Il Forteto one sunny Tuesday in April 1998. We spent most of the day watching milk warm, settle, drain, and become hand-formed delicacies for the table. Some cheeses were aged in ashes, others in crushed tomatoes, and others still in a seal of olive oil, salt, and pepper.

At Il Forteto, continual checks are made on the cheese for correct acid-to-base balance. Photograph by Eric Schreiber.

The people who make it all happen at Il Forteto make the cheese, watch the seasons, raise their children, and farm the land in concert with nature. Their extraordinary product bears witness to their willingness to give everything its season. We went to Vicchio to learn about making sheep's milk cheese, and we did. We also came away with a much deeper appreciation of the power of simplicity.

Salting cheese began with the Romans, who found that the salt allowed them to store cheese longer and discouraged contamination; here an early twentieth-century Wisconsin cheese maker carries on the practice. Photograph courtesy of State Historical Society of Wisconsin.

Members of the Cheese Carriers Guild at the cheese market in Alkmaar, The Netherlands, carry on a tradition that dates to the Middle Ages. The guild was formally founded by 1619. Today the carriers, who wear straw hats that match the colors of their warehouse company, must serve a two-year apprenticeship. They are responsible for ferrying the cheese back and forth from the Waagsquare to the weighmasters, who keep the sellers honest. Photograph courtesy of VVV Alkmaar en Omstreken (Alkmaar Tourist Information Office).

By about the first century A.D., cheese makers had mastered the techniques of both short-term and long-term storage, and probably at about this time they began to increase their knowledge of the process of fermentation. The principle that applied to controlling fermentation in wine could also in many ways serve the maker of cheese. But centuries before European monasteries turned cheese making into a large-scale production, Roman cheese makers added a critical step to the process—adding rennet, which forces coagulation. Virgil described rennet being added to pots of soft cheese and allowed to set overnight.

By adding rennet, either from plants or calves, the Romans developed the technique for stabilizing and pressing curds, creating a bridge to hard-cheese production. Of course, the Romans' general preoccupation with the good life encouraged improvements in cheese making and increased consumption, at all stages of curing. They, among other inhabitants of the Mediterranean and central Europe, literally ate their way into the Middle Ages.

Medieval Europe

During the Middle Ages, the Scandinavians churned milk into butter as well as into an early form of kefir (fermented cow's milk). In France, Burgundians thrived on soft herb cheese as well as bloomy (smooth, white-crusted) varieties such as Brie. (Brie was not called that until 1876, when it was named for the district in France in which it became popular.) And while France's emperor Charlemagne rode across the plains to advance his political purposes, he also scanned the countryside for fine cheese, acquainting himself with the delights of France's pungent blue Roquefort, among others. Centuries of family tradition had instilled in Charlemagne a love for cheese, as well as a longing to enjoy and pass along the varieties prized by his ancestors. (Some say that his love for cheese surpassed his passion for women and fine wine.)

Benedictine monks had established a thriving cluster of monasteries, where men divided their days between prayer, text and Bible reading, working the fields, and making cheese. Cheese was the staple of the monastic diet, very practical for a frugal existence within cool, damp walls.

The countries of the Mediterranean continued to produce fine cheese from ewe's and goat's milk. (Cattle never migrated far enough south to overtake the indigenous population of livestock.) The hot, dryer weather of southern Italy and Greece provided the perfect moisture balance for curing and aging, processes that there required far less salt than the amounts used by artisans in northern Europe. Reggiano Parmesan appeared in Emilia Romano, in the Lombardy region of northern Italy. Because cheese making remained a community activity, the process remained controlled, surviving relatively unscathed and consistent for centuries.

France and the British Isles

During the Hundred Years' War (1337–1453), the hooves of the armies' horses shredded farms in France and the British Isles that had finally stabilized after years of nurturing. Less produce meant less food for livestock, as well as for farmers, who were eager to trade their sheep and cows for money, dry goods, and textiles. Goats, however, largely kept by the peasants, remained prolific. Those hearty creatures, survivors of rocky coastlines and sparsely grassed fields, needed no nurturing. Herds of goats provided milk that kept whole villages from starving to death.

Parmesan Meets Prosciutto

The Emilia-Romagna region of northern Italy can claim two great, and complementary, delicacies. For more than 700 years, the region has produced great cheese; here cheese makers developed and nurtured the now world-famous Parmigiano Reggiano.

The thrifty farmers of the northern Italian commune of Parma have for years fed their pigs the warm whey that comes from the day's cheese yield. From these pigs come cured hams—prosciutto—that taste like no others on Earth.

Take a tip from these knowledgeable Italians: Parmesan tastes best when cut and served after six months to two years of aging. Because cheese continually undergoes a drying-out process, Parmesan aged past two years tends to get brittle and hard to cut or grate. As much as the Italians honor their antiquities, they know that older isn't always better, especially with cheese.

Long-time makers of cheese from all-natural fresh milk, the Amish in the United States are descendants of a group that broke away from the Swiss Mennonites in the 1690s.
Photograph ©LeeAnne Martin.

Some century and a half later, in Restoration France, cheese production once again hummed, and late in the 1700s, in a village in Normandy called Camembert, another great cheese was born.

In England, cheese has been produced for more than 2,000 years. (This is not surprising, given that the Romans had traveled in that country since approximately A.D. 55.) The 1800s brought renewed cheese-making enthusiasm, and hard cheese became a solid part of British tradition. Cheese making continued as a farmhouse activity until the late 1800s, when kitchen and small factory production grew to a much larger scale. English cheeses were named for the regions in which they were produced—Cheshire, Cheddar, Derby, and Stilton.

The town of Cheddar, in Somerset, brought forth its first cheese by that name sometime during the mid-1500s. A popular tourist haven because of its deep scenic chasms and falls, Cheddar also offered visitors the chance to buy a little fine cheese from its vendors. While the first settlers from England were making their way to the shores of North America, the town of Stilton, in Huntingdonshire, began to earn its place in cheese tradition. Commonly referred to as the king of cheeses, the blue-veined Stilton fast became a British favorite. Unique in texture, with a rich flavor combination of cheddar and blue mold, Stilton offers a gastronomical experience that has made it a favorite worldwide.

Caerfilly was first perfected in 1831 in Cardiff, Wales, where it is known as miner's cheese to this day, because underground workers survived on it for months. This traditional Welsh cheese has an outer crust that locks in the right amount of moisture, making it a good candidate for long-term storage.

The United States

Cheese making in North America, and specifically in the United States, also remained a farmhouse process throughout the seventeenth and eighteenth centuries. Dairies and kitchens produced cheese for sale, but in rounds weighing no more than twenty to thirty pounds.

However, by 1851, Rome, New York, entrepreneur Jesse Williams had built the first U.S. cheese factory and introduced production on a grand scale. After extensive experimentation, Williams regulated the timing as well as the temperature for converting milk to curds, regardless of volume. Major processing plants began to spring up nationwide.

Today, in North America, a bounty of cheese awaits us at the market, in specialty shops, and through mail-order suppliers. It comes from all corners of the globe—North American Cheddar, blue-veined Roquefort from France, Stilton from Britain, and raclette from Switzerland. From central Europe and Greece come sheep and goat Feta, from Spain, golden Mahon and zesty Manchego. We enjoy Gouda from Holland and Gjetost from Norway.

In more than three out of five countries in the world, cheese is a part of life. More than fifty countries export cheese; the major contributors are France, Germany, Italy, Great Britain, and Switzerland. France alone claims more than 280 varieties of cheese from cows, sheep, and goats, including at least a dozen varieties of Brie.

But while commercial purveyors deliver countless varieties of cheese almost to our door, the satisfaction that comes from making our own cheese in our own kitchens remains as great as it must have been for the first cheese maker on earth.

A typical Vermont small-farm milking scene, probably early in the twentieth century. Photograph courtesy of Vermont Historical Society.

Shelving Provolone in Wisconsin today.
Photograph courtesy of WISCONSIN MILK MARKETING BOARD.

the craft of making great cheese at home

EVEN IF YOU SURRENDER HOURS to warming and ripening milk, and sometimes months to curing and aging your cheeses, the results are well worth the wait. Fresh cheese is full of nutrition; its flavor surpasses that of most commercial varieties. Homemade cream cheese, for instance, remains full of flavor, yet delightfully free of the coloring, chemicals, and gum added to commercial cream cheese. Chevre (goat cheese) from your kitchen, one of the simplest to make, puts commercial varieties to shame. And once mold growth begins on your homemade Stilton, you'll see day-to-day progress in the development of its blue striations.

Making cheese doesn't need to be complicated or costly. Most soft cheeses simply require good milk, bacteria, enzymes, and time. A Stilton or a Cheddar takes practice; start with a simple cheese and savor the flavor as well as the fun of making it.

From Milk to Cheese: The Basic Process

Whether you're making soft or hard cheeses, with cow's, goat's, or sheep's milk, the basic series of steps remains the same. Casein, fat, bacteria starters, and rennet work hand in hand to produce a mass of delicious curds ready for the mold, cheesecloth, or press. Since every cheese starts with identical basic elements (milk, heat, bacteria, and rennet), how can the cheese-making process produce such a grand variety of results?

The hundreds of cheeses develop their characteristic textures, flavors, and appearance from different combinations of time, temperature, bacterial cultures, and enzymes. A mesophilic (medium-temperature) culture and rennet (which contains the enzyme that encourages milk to curdle) form the basis for Cheddar, Feta, and cottage cheese. A thermophilic (high-temperature) culture and rennet create both Swiss and Parmesan cheese. The fungi *penicillium roqueforti* generates cheeses such as Stilton and Danish Blue. Factor in the effects of time, type of milk, and amount of rennet or other enzyme, and you've accounted for the delectable variations.

The World Championship Cheese Contest

Since 1957, Madison, Wisconsin, has hosted the annual Olympics of cheesedom—the World Championship Cheese Contest, sponsored by the Wisconsin Cheese Makers Association. On their way to selection as Best of Class, the entrants—true cheeses and butters—start with 100 points. As the cheeses make their way past the judges, points may be deducted for defects in flavor, body and texture, salt, color, finish, and—where appropriate—packaging. The Best in Class finalists enter an ultimate round of tasting and testing, which identifies the World Champion Cheese.

In 1998, 800 cheeses competed, entered by cheese makers from New York to Seattle, New South Wales to Helsinki. The champion, with a score of 99.257, was Per Olesen's "Olesen's Danablu," from Denmark. A heartbreakingly close runner-up, with 99.225, was Vermont cheese maker Marcel Gravel's Cheddar. Other winners in various classes included cheeses from Wisconsin (Provolone), Switzerland (Swiss-style), Idaho (Colby-Jack), British Columbia (Aged Cheddar), and Washington (Aged Goat's Milk).

When you're ready to enter the contest with your prize cheese, get in touch with the Wisconsin Cheese Makers Association. In the meantime, for up-to-the-minute cheese news, you might want to join the American Cheese Society in Darien, Wisconsin (www.cheesesociety.org; or phone 414.728.4458).

Shelving Cheddar at a Wisconsin cheese factory.
Photograph courtesy of WISCONSIN MILK MARKETING BOARD.

Mixing starter and milk for a homemade starter culture

Less is more when adding cheese coloring.

Dry rennet tablet, quartered and powdered

cheese bit…

When you add coloring to cheese, a little goes a long way. Not necessarily because you'll end up with bright orange cheese, but because too much enthusiasm in coloring will break down the fermentation process and the curds.

The chain of events for all cheese, whether soft or hard, fresh or aged, looks like this:

1 WARMING AND SOURING THE MILK. Fresh, pasteurized milk is warmed to a temperature that encourages live bacteria to interact with the protein, fat, minerals, and vitamins in the milk. At this point, bacterial culture (either powdered or fresh) can be gently stirred into the milk—this is called the "starter culture." It gets the whole process of controlled fermentation going, and the natural souring process known as acidification now begins: acid forms as bacteria engulf and break down the lactose (milk sugars). Souring takes from one to fifteen hours, depending on the cheese. Because movement and changes in temperature can upset the growth of bacteria, *it's best not to move the milk pot once the process starts.*

For hard varieties of cheese, annatto (coloring), spice, herbs, and flavor enzymes (such as lipase for Parmesan) are added at this stage, after the starter culture.

2 ADDING RENNET. Rennet, a milk-curdling substance, comes in either powdered or liquid form. Rennet introduces an enzyme that works with the starter culture to move the process of acidifying the milk along. The enzymes force the acid to clot, or curdle. In the curdling process, some protein, fat, and other solids bond with each other to form *curds*, separating from the water and other protein, or the *whey*. The rennet causes the cultured milk to set, producing a ripened, soft curd.

The journey from milk to renneted, ready-to-cut curds requires variable times and temperatures, depending on the cheese. Balance is the key here. The milk needs to be warm, but not too warm; the right amount of rennet needs to be added; and the whole blend needs to set. If any part of the process is rushed or overdone, the results are likely to be disappointing.

3 **SEPARATING CURDS AND WHEY.** For fresh cheeses and a variety of softer cheeses, curds are cut and allowed to set and settle as the whey rises to the surface. The curds are then drained, molded, or both, usually for ten hours or overnight. A soft cheese, such as a cottage cheese or ricotta, gets drained, then transferred to a bowl or to the refrigerator. Others, such as a chevre, get drained, perhaps salted, then often transferred to a mold for settling and shaping.

4 **ADDING SALT.** A bit of flake salt is usually added to soft as well as hard cheese at this point. With its alkaline base, salt is a key factor in slowing down or halting the acidification (souring) or fermentation process; it removes excess tang and adds a little creaminess.

For most fresh and soft cheeses, the process stops here.

Ripening and aging aren't necessary for all cheeses. If you allow a fresh batch of soft cheese to rest in the refrigerator even overnight, your mascarpone, ricotta, or cream cheese gains plenty of residual flavor. *For hard and mold-ripened cheeses, the chain of events continues.*

After crushing, dry rennet needs to be mixed with cool water.

cheese bit...

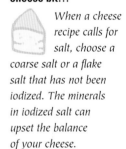
When a cheese recipe calls for salt, choose a coarse salt or a flake salt that has not been iodized. The minerals in iodized salt can upset the balance of your cheese.

Both chèvre, *left*, and ricotta, *right*, continue to drain for several hours in their molds and shrink considerably before they are ready to chill.

WHY COLLECT WHEY?

Because milk is about 90 percent liquid, you will have whey in abundance. If you want to collect it for making cheese such as ricotta and Gjetost, plan ahead. Whey needs to be used while it is still warm (so the enzymes are active).

You can also refrigerate whey and use it later to give baked goods like bread, biscuits, and pizza dough a richer flavor and tang.

A variety of hard cheeses, such as this sage Cheddar, need a bit of salt rubbed into the surface before they are waxed and aged.

Cutting the curds, still unseparated from the watery whey

Once molded and pressed, the cheese is firm and easy to handle

5 **CUTTING AND DRAINING THE CURDS.** Cutting the curds promotes the release of whey, which in turn encourages the curds to form a dryer, solid mass that will cure in one block. Cutting also contributes to balance, since plenty of whey still needs to be removed. Once curds are cut, most of the remaining whey floats to the surface. This makes draining off excess liquid and stirring easier.

6 **FOREWORKING THE CURDS.** Foreworking is the proper cheese-making term for stirring renneted curds to expel or separate additional whey from the curds before they are heated.

7 **COOKING THE CURDS.** Heating and stirring the curds rids them of even more whey and firms them up. If curds for hard cheese lack body, they can't come together as one unit; they will simply fall apart in the press. Curds need to be soft enough to bond, and springy enough to provide structure.

8 **MOLDING AND PRESSING THE CURDS.** This step gives structure and an additional squeeze to the cheese. Shaping a harder cheese may take several days, during which the cheese is frequently flipped from one side to the other to distribute the internal moisture evenly. (Otherwise, half of the cheese can be moist while half remains a bit dry.)

At this point, mold-ripened cheeses like brick, Camembert, and Stilton can be injected with additional bacteria for ripening and set aside to air dry in preparation for aging.

9 DRYING. Most hard cheese requires a little time on the rack or mat, at room temperature, after pressing. Cheeses such as Gouda, Cheddar, Swiss, and others that do not mold ripen can be waxed and stored at cool temperatures for aging. Others, such as Parmesan, can be left to continue to form a natural rind—in some cases, cheese can be rubbed with a little olive oil to seal in the moisture and keep the rind supple.

10 AGING. Whether it's a ripe Camembert, a creamy Brie, or a tangy Feta, more time means more taste. (Making cheese is much like making a rich soup or infused oil; the flavor intensifies and texture increases with a little steeping time.) Temperature and humidity are critical factors in the aging process. Whether you make a soft, mold-ripened, or hard cheese, you'll need a hygrometer (a humidity-measuring instrument) to get a daily reading of the climate of your refrigerator or cool room.

A handmade Gouda air dries on a cheese mat to form a natural rind before receiving a coat of red wax.

Some cheeses, such as this Stilton, require aging in order to develop their characteristic flavor and texture.

cheese bit…

If you'd like to learn more about cheese in general, a specific type of cheese, or Americans who make it, get in touch with the American Cheese Society in Darien, Wisconsin. Members receive event information, as well as a directory of artisans who participate. The highlight of the ACS year is a conference with sessions on such topics as "What's Going On with Organic?" "What Do People Do with Cheese, Anyway?" "Cheese, Wine, and Beer Pairings," and "Cheesemaking 101."

Getting Started

Making great cheese requires absolutely clean working conditions, fresh ingredients, and patience. Chances are that if you want to make cheese, you already enjoy spending time in your kitchen. Without knowing it, you may also already have a number of cheese-making utensils stashed in your drawers and cabinets. In case you don't, all are available from commercial sources (check the sources on page 136). Nonporous or "food-grade" plastic containers, as well as good-quality stainless-steel utensils and equipment, are available in many supermarkets and discount stores. Your equipment needs to be reliable, not expensive. (Early cheese makers didn't have gourmet cooking stores.)

You'll need a good-quality thermometer, double boilers (more than one, if you expect to make more than one batch of cheese at a time), and a quality cheese press. While you can get by with a few home-made items, you may want to seriously consider investing in a commercial press, which has a set of pressure gauges as well as uniform molds. Good equipment not only will last a lifetime but will give you ongoing consistent results—very important if you intend to make cheese more than a few times.

If you are not sure whether you want to make cheese for years to come, you can experiment with a number of soft cheeses before getting into more advanced production. For soft cheeses you don't need to invest in much equipment. However, if you make a few hard cheeses and you're hooked, go ahead and make the investment in a press, even if you create reasonable homemade substitutes for other items.

Clean Working Conditions

You need to sterilize or clean your cheese-making equipment and kitchen countertops with hot water. To destroy unwanted bacteria and avoid contamination, be sure to sterilize your utensils each time before you use them. You can keep a pot of water simmering for sterilizing long-handled spoons, whisks, and curd knives. Just remember not to boil plastic or allow plastic utensils to simmer in hot water for more than five minutes.

You can either sterilize molds, colanders, and cheese-press parts in the dishwasher, or scald them. Cheesecloths and mats can also be scalded or rinsed with hot water in the dishwasher. You don't need to use bleach, soap, or disinfectants. As a matter of fact, they can interfere with the chemistry of the cheese-making process, and your cheese may fail. If you choose to use soap, be sure to rinse everything thoroughly. If you use bleach, use dairy bleach such as sodium hypochlorite and again be sure that everything is thoroughly rinsed.

Use bowls, pans, and other utensils made only of glass, stainless steel, plastic labeled "food grade," or another galvanized or nonporous material. Avoid any substance or surface that is porous, because it can absorb liquid. In porous utensils, bacteria may sneak in and propagate, contaminating and sometimes spoiling the curds. *Poor hygiene and unsanitary conditions can produce not only a bitter cheese, but an unhealthy one. The propagation of bacteria, especially in certain molds, could send you to the emergency room.*

Stainless steel is the material of choice for cheese-making utensils, bowls, and plates, although glass, food-grade plastic, or another nonporous material is certainly acceptable.

Supplies and Equipment

SUPPLIES

- Mats or small towels for air drying cheese

- Cheesecloth or buttercloth, for draining and handling cheese

- Wax, if you plan to wax your cheese (You usually have a choice of red, yellow, or black.)

EQUIPMENT
(preferably stainless steel, when available)

- Curd knife, for cutting curds

- Long-handled slotted spoons and ladles, for stirring

- Whisks, for stirring and turning curds

- Dairy thermometer. I prefer the kind with a long stem that clips to the side of the double boiler. A good dairy thermometer is gauged to read temperatures from 20 to 220°F.

- Standard measuring spoons

- Dry and liquid measuring cups

- Spray bottles, if you plan to make mold-ripened cheeses

- Molds, for chèvre, Camembert, and other soft cheeses. Use stainless steel or food-grade (nonporous) plastic molds.

- Food-grade baskets, if you plan to make ricotta or other loosely curdled cheese

- Large basins or bowls, for collecting the whey from cheese draining in the colander. They should be able to accommodate 1½ gallons of hot whey.

- Shallow draining pans for collecting whey; I use 9 x 9 or 9 x 12 cake pans.

- Cheese boards, for draining cheeses such as Brie or Camembert. These allow the molded cheese to rest and continue to drain without sitting in a pool of its own whey.

- Colanders. Enamel or stainless steel work best.

- Large pots and double boilers (Most cheeses require at least one and frequently two gallons of milk.)

- Cheese press, to supply pressure and shape to drained curds (see "About Cheese Presses" on page 31).

Shelbyville-Shelby County
Public Library

Basic Ingredients

MILK

Fresh ingredients, particularly fresh milk, lay the foundation for quality cheese. The best-tasting cheeses are made from raw, organic milk, unpasteurized and unhomogenized (see "How to Pasteurize Raw Milk" on this page). Homogenizing tends to break down the fat particles in milk, which makes them more likely to dissipate when the milk is warmed or stirred. This results in a softer, less sturdy cheese. Cheese made from the homogenized milk you buy at a large dairy or supermarket may not be quite as flavorful and could well be a little softer than cheese made from nonhomogenized milk—but rest assured it will still be great cheese.

You'll be pleased to know that many of the nutrients in milk get passed along when you make cheese. The curds contain healthy amounts of vitamins A, D, E, and K. The whey offers a bounty of B-complex vitamins as well vitamin C. Both contain protein. About 90 percent of milk is water. In most cases, one gallon of whole milk will produce roughly one pound of cheese.

For most people in the United States, cow's milk is more available than milk from goats and sheep. However, each animal's milk produces cheese with a signature flavor and aroma. If you can locate a dairy farmer, learn the times for milking, and plan ahead, you can have fresh, raw milk.

Cows usually produce two to six gallons of milk daily; goats yield between a half gallon and a little more than a gallon; and sheep give only small quantities of milk each day, about a quart per ewe. The fat content in sheep's milk exceeds that of cow's and goat's. Sheep's milk contains 9 percent fat, goat's milk 6 percent fat, and cow's milk 3.8–4 percent fat.

cheese bit…

Whether you are pasteurizing milk or warming milk to make cheese, take your time. The ingredients need to reach the desired temperature very gradually. Quick heating kills important bacteria, fat, and enzymes that turn milk into cheese.

HOW TO PASTEURIZE RAW MILK

1 Slowly heat the milk in a double boiler until it reaches a uniform temperature of 144–145°F.

2 Hold it at this temperature for 30 minutes. To avoid a rise in temperature, you may need to lower the heat under the double boiler, or turn it off completely.

3 Remove the heated milk from the burner and cool it immediately in a basin or sink of ice or ice water. Allow the temperature to drop to 40°F.

4 Use the pasteurized milk immediately, or refrigerate it for future use.

It's About Milk
(and Moving to Lapland)

As much as timing, patience, coagulation, and ripening contribute to cheese making, the fat content of the milk base probably plays the most critical role in flavor and texture.

In most countries, cheese is commonly made from the milk of indigenous or widely available animals. In the United States, for instance, cheese comes mostly from the milk of cows, goats, sheep, and buffalo. Cow's milk contains roughly 3.8–3.9 percent fat; goat and buffalo milk, approximately 6 percent; and sheep's milk, 9 percent. In other countries, the milk of yaks, camels, and reindeer provide the source of cheese.

According to food historian Waverly Root, probably the richest and most nutritious milk available is reindeer milk, which contains about 22.5 butterfat and 10.3 percent protein (compared to cow's milk, with 3 percent protein.) Root credits reindeer milk with contributing directly to the stamina and good health of Laplanders.

One reason we don't find reindeer cheese even in the elite markets of other countries is, perhaps, that during the height of the milking season, reindeer give only about 1½ cups of milk daily.

Photograph courtesy of National Park Service Carl Sandburg Home National Historic Site.

Photograph by Elise Smith, courtesy of U.S. Fish and Wildlife Service.

Photograph by Ron Singer, courtesy of U.S. Fish and Wildlife Service.

STARTER CULTURES

Bacterial cultures, each with its characteristic response to heat and milk, act as catalysts in the acidification, or souring, process. Since they are what start warm milk curdling, or forming curds, they are called *starter cultures*. Each starter culture has a different level of heat sensitivity, which makes it important to watch the temperature gauge when using them and warming the milk.

The two main types of starter culture are named for the amount of heat they need to start the curdling process: mesophilic (requiring low or medium temperatures) and thermophilic (requiring higher temperatures).

Mesophilic bacteria cultures work best when milk and curds warm to no higher than 103–110°F after pasteurization. Mesophilic cultures produce a number of soft and hard cheeses, such as cottage cheese, cream cheese, Cheddar, Feta, and Gouda. Thermophilic cultures can withstand greater heat, and the organisms continue to be active in acidification in temperatures up to 130–132°F after pasteurization.

You can buy starter cultures as premeasured direct-set powder (which contains rennet) and store them in the freezer for two to three months. With these commercially prepared cultures, you will get extremely reliable results, and they take the worry out of measuring, or depending on a cooked variety. However, homemade starter cultures are relatively simple to cook up. They keep well in the refrigerator for two to three days, or in the freezer for several weeks (see "Making Your Own Starter" on page 29).

Dry direct-set cultures are a commercial alternative to making your own culture.

Here are some of my experiences of what can go wrong working with starter cultures:

NO CURDS WILL FORM (TOO LITTLE ACIDITY): If your milk doesn't reach the proper acidity, or doesn't begin to form curds, you may have used inactive bacteria or poor milk or milk inoculated with antibiotics.

TOO MUCH ACIDITY: Using too much starter culture can create too much acidity too quickly; the excess acidity will produce a bitter cheese.

TOO MUCH ACIDITY, TOO MUCH MOISTURE, OR BOTH: If you allow your milk to ripen longer (30 minutes or more) than the recipe advises, you can also create too much acidity and too much moisture.

In any of these cases, you can try either cooking the curds a little longer or adding a bit of flake salt—either may alter the fermentation enough to balance things out. If neither works, I start over with a fresh batch of milk.

Too much coloring and too little acid will produce curds that lack the texture and body needed for cutting the mass of drained curds into slices.

MAKING YOUR OWN STARTER

INGREDIENTS AND EQUIPMENT

- 1 quart of skim milk
- ½ teaspoon or packet of freeze-dried starter culture
- 2 pint jars, or 1 quart jar, and lids, sterilized and cooled to room temperature

METHOD

Pour the skim milk into the pint jars or quart jar, filling each to approximately ½ inch from the rim. Screw on the sterilized lid, then simmer in a hot water bath for 30–40 minutes. Remove the jar from the bath and allow it to cool.

Mesophilic starter requires a milk cooled to 70–72°F. Thermophilic starter requires milk cooled to 108–110°F.

Once the milk has reached the desired temperature (measured with a dairy thermometer), stir in the starter culture, and screw the lid back onto the jar. Swirl the jar gently for a minute or two to blend the culture and the milk.

Place the cultured milk in a warm (72°F), draft-free spot and allow it to ripen for 24 hours.

To test for success, remove the lid. The culture should have the consistency of a thick yogurt, and slide away from the sides of the jar easily. The culture should also have a sweet, slightly tangy flavor. To store, either refrigerate, or spoon the finished culture into sterile ice cube trays and freeze for future use. It will keep for two to three days in the refrigerator and up to ninety days in the freezer.

cheese bit…

Americans eat more than thirty-six pounds of cheese per capita each year, and they eat more Cheddar and mozzarella than any other varieties. In my view, this directly correlates to the American appetite for grilled-cheese sandwiches and pizza. Definitely a maybe.

Step 1: Simmer the milk in a hot-water bath.

Step 2: Remove the milk from the bath and allow it to cool.

Step 3: Add a dry packet of your favorite starter to the milk, replace the lid, and allow to ripen.

RENNET

You will add rennet, an enzyme, to ripened milk after you have added the starter culture. Rennet is available in liquid as well as tablet form, and you should probably try both. Altitude, humidity, and temperature can all affect the capacity of cheese to coagulate, that is, thicken into a mass. Although the choice of dry or liquid rennet should make no difference in the cheese-making process, it may—and you should use the variety that adapts to your needs.

It is important not to rush the renneting process or to apply more rennet than a recipe calls for. There are no shortcuts when making cheese, and balance is critical to a quality cheese. So take your time, and make moderation your watchword.

Here are some educational experiences from my kitchen concerning rennet. In every case, I've found it's best to simply start over.

SOFT OR SPONGY CURDS: These disappointing curds can be a result of too little rennet, poor-quality rennet, or old rennet.

RIPENED MILK REFUSES TO COAGULATE (HOLD TOGETHER): Using warm water will destroy the suspension structure of this enzyme, and your ripened milk will not coagulate. *Always blend rennet with cool water.*

HARD CURDS, GRAINY CURDS, OR BITTER CHEESE: Too much rennet.

cheese bit…

According to the American Cheese Society, the best place to store cheese is in the fruit-and-vegetable bin, on the shelf directly above it, or in the refrigerator door. Don't store it near the freezer compartment or meat bin, or it might freeze.

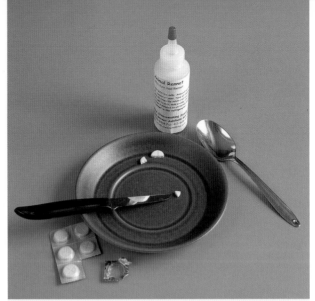
Rennet, in tablet and liquid form—it's a matter of preference.

RENNET

If no one had discovered rennet, we would all be encouraging our curdled cheese to coagulate by adding lemon juice or vinegar, which do the job but not as quickly.

The 1500s brought the revelation of what rennet could do, as its use became more refined. Five hundred years ago, the dairy farmer or cottage cheese maker extracted the fourth stomach from a newly slaughtered, once healthy, milk-fed calf. The fourth stomach, which contained the rennin, was then carefully washed and hung to dry in the air. The farmer added dehydrated pieces of the stomach directly to curdled milk, which solidified into a mass ready for the next step in the cheese-making process.

As we have learned to control certain bacteria that provoke deterioration, renneting has undergone a variety of purification procedures. Today cheese makers can buy dry rennet tablets or liquid rennet; vegetable rennet is available for vegetarians. No more pieces of dehydrated calf's stomach for us.

ABOUT CHEESE PRESSES

The cheese press is the one essential device for making hard cheese. You can assemble a homemade cheese press from wood, weights, and gallon containers; the difficulty lies in achieving the correct amount of pressure and good balance. I recommend a commercial press, if you want to be sure of a consistent product.

Commercial presses are easy to assemble as well as use. As with any other piece of equipment, you need to choose the press that you are most comfortable using. If possible, try a test run before making a purchase. The following are probably the three most reliable presses available for beginner and intermediate cheese makers (for sources, see page 136).

THE WHEELER PRESS is handcrafted from stainless steel and hardwood. It is very sturdy and will last as long you make cheese. It comes with pressure gauges, a stainless-steel mold, drip tray, separating disk, and followers. Although this is the most expensive of the three presses (about $200), it is one of the finest made and produces consistent, reliable cheeses properly pressed and evenly shaped. Its mold accommodates a three- to four-pound cheese, and the press supplies up to fifty pounds of pressure.

THE ITALIAN CHEESE PRESS also comes with a stainless-steel mold, drip tray, and separating disk, for about $120. It offers a convenient double basket for containing curds and draining whey, which the Wheeler does not. This press is also sturdy and provides consistently smooth-sided cheese. The cheese mold holds up to a two-pound cheese, and the press supplies up to fifty pounds of pressure.

THE DUTCH CHEESE PRESS is the largest press of the three at 19½" long, 9" wide, and 26¼" high. It makes a bigger cheese—up to ten pounds—and sells for about $100. Handcrafted of hardwood in the United States, it can supply up to 100 pounds of pressure. A cheese mold must be purchased separately.

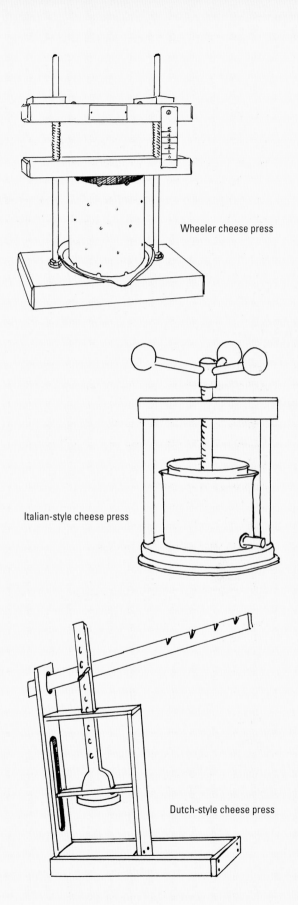

Wheeler cheese press

Italian-style cheese press

Dutch-style cheese press

thirty great cheeses to make at home

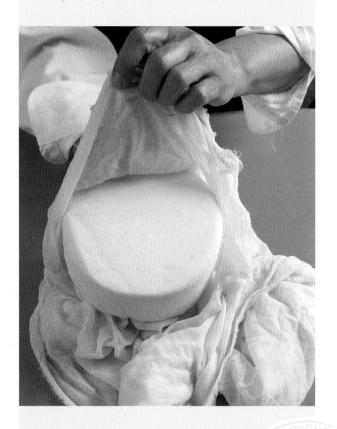

WITH THESE THIRTY RECIPES, you're on your way to making a wonderful variety of delicious cheeses in your kitchen. I hope that they reflect at least some of my own enthusiasm for cheese making, and that they will inspire you and encourage you to experiment as you gain assurance as a cheese maker. You'll find many great favorites, like Cheddar, cream cheese, and Stilton...some cheeses you may be less familiar with, like queso blanco or mascarpone...and at least an exciting few you have never heard of, perhaps Gjetost or Leipäjuusto.

I have ordered the cheese recipes roughly by the skill level required to make them with some confidence, beginning with the simplest. If you are making cheese for the first time, I recommend starting with a few soft cheeses, such as herb garden cheese and chèvre.

Develop your cheese-making technique with these and other soft varieties—mascarpone, ricotta, and queso blanco or perhaps cottage cheese. Among the soft cheeses, mozzarella and weinkase (wine cheese) take the most time and careful watching.

Once you're an old hand with the softer cheeses, venture into the hard varieties. These cheeses, such as Cheddar, Muenster, Gouda, or Feta, involve more steps in the making and more time than softer cheeses. Try a batch of baby Swiss and watch the "eyes" (the holes) appear right before yours. Or watch your first batch of Feta transform into a solid white mound as it drains.

the cheeses

FRESH, SOFT, AND SEMISOFT CHEESES

Fromage Blanc
Chèvre
Mascarpone
Herb Garden Cheese
Finnish Leipäjuusto
Cream Cheese
Cottage Cheese
Queso Blanco
Whole-Cream Ricotta
Whey Ricotta
Mozzarella
Stuffed Mozzarella
Braided Mozzarella
Scamorze (Smoked Mozzarella)
Weinkase

MOLD- AND AGE-RIPENED CHEESES

Stilton
All-American Brick
Danish Blue
Camembert

AGE-RIPENED HARD CHEESES

Muenster
Feta
White Goat Cheddar
Yellow Aged Cheddar
Sage Cheddar
Holland Gouda
Romano
Parmesan
Raclette
Baby Swiss
Gjetost

Based on my own experience, I advise you to hold off for awhile on making mold-ripened cheeses, such as Camembert, Stilton, or brick. Considerable time and practice go into getting the flavors and textures of these cheeses just right, as my first Stilton taught me. Hoping to speed up the mold-forming process, I added more bacteria than I needed. It worked all too well. What should have stretched over two or three weeks occurred almost overnight. The mold grew so fast and thick, it smothered the cheese and couldn't develop those lovely blue veins throughout. I had to start over.

So I don't expect every batch of cheese to be perfect. But you're much more likely to turn out delicious mozzarella or Danish blue later if you start with the softer types to gain experience and confidence. Get acquainted with how easily milk ripens, how simply you can encourage it to settle into curds. Learning to make cheese reminds me of learning to play the piano. You practice on the simple tunes—or recipes—until your patience wears thin as a sliver of Muenster. Then one day you find a glorious fugue rippling out from under your fingers—or a golden Cheddar aging perfectly in your pantry.

Cheese makers line up at the Mozzarella Company, a tiny cheese factory in downtown Dallas, to demonstrate the steps in making mozzarella, from chopping the curds to forming the fresh cheese into balls—all by hand. Owner Paula Lambert, *rear*, learned the process at a tiny Italian cheese factory, then founded the company in 1982.
Photograph courtesy of Mozzarella Company.

Tips on Milk

Heating times, cooling, and renneting vary, depending on the type of milk you decide to use, as well as the altitude and humidity of your area. (They behave differently, for instance, if you live in humid, sea-level Miami than if you live in dry, mile-high Denver.)

Cow's, sheep's, and goat's milk contain different amounts of protein, fat, and lactose. They react differently to heat, climate, and various bacterial cultures, which accounts for the varied flavor and texture of your homemade cheese.

Every recipe here calls for pasteurized milk. (Many cheese makers will argue that the best-tasting cheese comes from raw organic milk that has been pasteurized just before use; in fact, many cheese recipes call for organic raw milk.) Check the labels on milk you buy at grocery and health-food stores and whole-food markets. They will tell you whether milk is pasteurized, ultrapasteurized, homogenized, or nonhomogenized, organic or not. (I must admit that I am partial to organic goat's milk, whose sweet flavor and thick, creamy consistency have made me a milk drinker after years of abstinence.)

I have used both homogenized and nonhomogenized milk with fairly reliable results. Homogenized milk makes a softer curd, however, which is something to watch out for if you decide to make a round of hard Romano, for instance. Ultrapasteurized milk will also probably result in a too-soft curd—and frustration for you. I avoid using it, and I suggest that you do too. If you plan to pasteurize raw milk, a little care in the kitchen will enable you to render a rich, flavorful cheese. If you purchase raw milk, follow the directions in "How to Pasteurize Raw Milk" on page 26.

Tips on Time

For each recipe, I suggest an approximate total processing time: This includes the time required for curdling and curing. The time you'll spend heating milk or pressing curds is usually less than thirty minutes. You can do your part, then walk away and allow the milk to work its magic without you. Given the right conditions and quality ingredients, cheese almost makes itself. You do the facilitating and the waiting.

A Cheese-Making Quest

Making cheese in your kitchen opens the door to a whole world of opportunities as well as adventures. For instance, unless you own a dairy, you may go on a search for raw milk. Cow's milk is usually quite plentiful, but raw goat's milk remains fairly seasonal and harder to find in quantity.

Goat's milk is worth tracking down. Not only does it make tasty bread and tangy cheese, it is a highly healthy food. Unlike cow's milk, it is naturally homogenized because its fat particles suspend naturally in the whey. It's also high in immune-system boosters, with fatty acids that combat gallstones, cystic fibrosis, and even coronary illness. Goat's milk also breaks down cholesterol and provides a delicious alternative for folks who can't digest the lactose in cow's milk.

Polly Fafatch of Lakehaven Farms.
Photograph by the author.

On my own search, I discovered Polly Fafach of Lakehaven Farms in Boulder, Colorado, along with fresh, creamy goat's milk, whey bread, and a recipe for Finnish Leipäjuusto. Polly and I found that we shared an enthusiasm for making cheese at home, a delight in ethnic tradition, and a love for goats. Try making a batch of Leipäjuusto from the recipe Polly passed on to me, which came to her from a friend from Finland, Pirkko O'Clock (see page 45).

According to Pirkko, Leipäjuusto is also known as bread cheese in Finland, because of its round, flat appearance. While it can be found in markets, most people make it at home, patting the drained curds into the shape of a flatbread and baking it on a wooden paddle that sits on the hot bricks or stones around an open fire.

fresh, soft, and semisoft cheeses

FROMAGE BLANC

Fromage blanc (French for *white cheese*) adds fresh flavor and nutrition to a variety of foods. It complements fruit, vegetables, pasta, and bread with equal ease. Don't let the rich, creamy consistency fool you—fromage blanc is relatively low in fat. I prefer to use whole organic cow's milk, but you can make it with skim milk, for an even lower-fat cheese. You'll appreciate fromage blanc as a simple and reliable cheese to make in the kitchen, one that combines well with other cheeses such as ricotta, cottage cheese, cream cheese, and even yogurt. An easy, elegant recipe to start with is the Fromage Strawberry Wreath on page 133, pictured here.

LEVEL
Very easy, a good first cheese to make

START TO FINISH
20–24 hours

BEST USE
Cold. Used as a spread, tossed into pasta, or served with fresh fruit or vegetables

STORAGE
Keeps well for 7–10 days refrigerated in an air-tight container

YIELD
2–2¼ pounds fromage blanc

For an interesting variation in flavor and texture, try blending:

1 cup fromage blanc
1 cup fresh cottage cheese
¼ cup fresh cream cheese

Blend thoroughly with a whisk or pulse in a blender or food processor for 2–3 seconds. Blend in a little honey for a slightly sweeter mixture. Serve this fromage-blanc blend with toasted almonds and fresh raspberries. Or garnish with herbs, for a tangy and refreshing accompaniment to fresh bread or warm muffins.

TIP... *Fromage blanc requires more time than handwork—it simply needs to sit and set. You can heat the milk and add the starter in the evening after dinner, let it set overnight, and easily finish by the next afternoon.*

INGREDIENTS

1 gallon whole organic cow's milk

½ teaspoon or packet fromage blanc or fromagina direct-set culture (both include starter and rennet)

HEATING AND COOLING THE MILK

Because the milk must cool quickly, fill a basin or sink with ice and water before the milk has finished heating.

In a double boiler, heat the milk for 20–30 minutes, until it reaches 170°F. Remove the pot of milk from the stove and place it immediately into the basin or sink of ice water. Leave the thermometer in the pot, and allow the milk to cool down to 70–72°F. You may need to add more ice to keep the water cold enough to reduce the temperature of the milk.

ADDING STARTER AND MAKING CURDS

Maintain a kitchen temperature of 70–72°F for best results when making curds. Transfer the milk to a draft-free spot in your kitchen, and slowly stir in the fromage starter culture. Cover the pot with a lid or clean kitchen towel and allow it to rest for 12–15 hours, or overnight.

DRAINING AND SETTLING THE CURDS

Place a colander in a basin for draining, and line the colander with a fine cheesecloth or buttercloth. Make sure the cloth is large enough to cover the curds once you have transferred them into the colander.

Use a large ladle to spoon the cheese curds into the colander. Bring the excess cloth over the curds to cover them, and allow them to drain for 8–12 hours, or until their consistency resembles that of cream cheese. Transfer to an airtight container and chill for 2–3 hours before serving.

CHÈVRE

Fromage de la chèvre, as the French call it—cheese made from goat's milk—is a thick, smooth, creamy cheese that brings nutrition and versatility to meals. It makes an excellent snack, by itself or with bread. Fresh, whole milk ensures fine flavor. Chèvre needs only a little salt to enhance its flavor, but you may choose to add minced fresh parsley, pepper, or a little freshly chopped chives for variety; I sprinkled the chèvre pictured here with fresh ground green peppercorns and herbs. For another family- and guest-pleasing treat, serve Chèvre Dill Muffins (page 123).

LEVEL
Easy, a good beginner cheese requiring little handwork

START TO FINISH
15–24 hours

BEST USE
Good table and cooking cheese

STORAGE
Keeps well for up to 2 weeks with refrigeration

YIELD
1–1¼ pounds chèvre

INGREDIENTS

- 1 gallon fresh raw whole goat's milk
- 1 packet direct-set chèvre starter culture (contains culture and rennet)
- ¼ teaspoon salt

Note: Chèvre molds are nice to have but not necessary for making this cheese.

TIPS... *The first time you make soft goat cheese, I recommend using a premeasured packet of direct-set starter culture, as this recipe calls for. Rennet is included in the mix.*

Start this cheese during late afternoon or early evening. The cultured milk can then take overnight to form a firm curd.

HEATING THE MILK

In a double boiler, heat the milk to 170°F (clip your dairy thermometer inside the upper pan). Immediately remove the pot of milk with the thermometer from the heat and place it in a sink of crushed ice or ice water. If you use ice, set the milk pot on a 2- to 3-inch bed of ice, and pack ice around the sides. If you use ice water, keep checking the temperature with your finger. If the water begins to feel warm, add more ice. Keep the conditions as cold as possible, reducing the temperature quickly to 70–72°F.

ADDING THE STARTER

Once the milk cools, place the pot on a toweled countertop or table. Gently stir in the starter with a wire whisk. Cover the pot with a kitchen towel and move it to a draft-free spot in your kitchen. Chèvre solidifies best at 68–70°F.

CURDLING TIME

Allow the chèvre to incubate for 12–15 hours. Your goal: a firm but not dense consistency; the curds often look and feel like a thick yogurt.

RIPENING TIME

Line a stainless-steel or enamel-coated colander with fine cheesecloth or buttercloth—or use cheese molds, which need no cheesecloth. Set the colander or molds in a basin or shallow pan, which will collect the whey.

Gently ladle all the curds into the colander. Cover the chèvre with a piece of cheesecloth or buttercloth and allow it to rest in the colander or molds for 6–8 hours.

If you used a colander: Transfer the chèvre to a bowl. Gently stir in the salt until the mixture is well blended. Cover and refrigerate.

If you used molds: Gently remove the molds and transfer the cheese to a shallow bowl or plate. Sprinkle the salt over the cheese and serve or refrigerate.

MASCARPONE

Although mascarpone (pronounced *mas-car-pō'-na*) often serves as the key ingredient in Italian desserts, its flavor and texture readily lend themselves to bread and grains. Toss it into pasta or blend it with peaches for an unforgettable trifle. Regardless of how you intend to serve this smooth, flavorful cheese, all you have to contribute are light cream, tartaric acid, and time—this cheese comes to life without rennet or starter. For an incredibly rich dessert, make the Tiramisu Tango on page 132 with your homemade mascarpone.

LEVEL
Easy

START TO FINISH
12–14 hours

BEST USE
Chilled, for table use and desserts

STORAGE
Keeps well for 10 days to 2 weeks with refrigeration

YIELD
About 1½ cups mascarpone

INGREDIENTS

- 1 quart table or light cream (not heavy cream)
- 1 rounded ¼ teaspoon tartaric acid

HEATING AND THICKENING THE CREAM

Heat the cream in a double boiler over low heat, until the temperature on your dairy thermometer, clipped to the side of the upper pan, reaches 170–175°F. Lower the heat under the double boiler, so that you barely maintain the temperature. Stir the tartaric acid into the cream with a wire whisk.

The hot cream should begin to thicken immediately. If it doesn't, add a pinch more of the tartaric acid and continue to blend the mixture for another 5–7 minutes, or until the cream is the consistency of warm, thick pudding. (Don't get carried away with the tartaric acid. The cream will thicken, but you may end up with a mascarpone that feels grainy, instead of smooth and creamy.)

DRAINING THE CURDS

Place a colander in a drain pan. Line the colander with enough cheesecloth or butter-cloth to cover the curds. Ladle the mascarpone curds into the colander and cover with the excess cloth. Allow the cheese to drain in the refrigerator overnight or for 12–15 hours.

REFRIGERATING AND SERVING

Transfer to an airtight container and refrigerate until ready to use.

LEVEL
Easy, with little handwork. However, maintain a kitchen temperature of 70–72°F for best results.

START TO FINISH
About 2 days

BEST USE
Fresh, used as a spread, or tossed with steamed vegetables or pasta

STORAGE
Keeps well in refrigerator for 10 days to 2 weeks

YIELD
12–16 ounces of garden cheese

HERB GARDEN CHEESE

This spreadable goat cheese requires time to set, but little hands-on time and less milk than other soft cheeses. It gains its bouquet of flavors from the addition of fresh dill, parsley, and chives. At our house, the cheese is a favorite in omelets and crepes, with baked potatoes, or spread on toast. It's a healthy, highly digestible cheese that marries well with grains, vegetables, and fruit.

INGREDIENTS

½ gallon raw goat's milk

1 ounce mesophilic starter culture

1 drop of liquid calf's rennet diluted
in ¼ cup cool water

FOR CHEESE IN A BOWL

1 teaspoon fresh chives, chopped

1 teaspoon fresh parsley, finely chopped

¼–½ teaspoon fresh dill, finely chopped

¼ teaspoon fine salt

FOR HERB CHEESE ROLLS

2 teaspoons fresh chives, chopped

2 teaspoons parsley, finely chopped

¼–½ teaspoon fresh dill, finely chopped

HEATING THE MILK

Overheating the milk is a danger, for this recipe requires only a medium-high temperature for acidification. Slowly heat the goat's milk to 70–72°F in a double boiler. When your dairy thermometer reads the proper temperature, remove the milk from the double boiler.

ADDING STARTER AND RENNET

For best results, maintain a kitchen temperature of 70–72°F Slowly stir in the starter and blend it throughout the milk. Add the diluted rennet and use a whisk to gently blend it into the mixture. Cover the pot with a lid or clean kitchen towel, and place it in a draft-free area of your kitchen.

CURDLING TIME

Allow the cheese 18–20 hours to set. Your goal: the consistency of pudding or a thick yogurt.

TIP... *While doubling cheese recipes is never recommended, you can heat and process batches of milk simultaneously, for special occasions and gift giving.*

TIP... *You may want to plan ahead for this cheese, because it requires 24 hours for coagulation and another day for draining.*

ROLLING IN HERBS OR MIXING IN HERBS

You can either roll the cheese in herbs, as in the photo, or blend in the herbs—now is the time to decide. Rolling in herbs has great visual appeal. *If you decide to create your own herb cheese rolls*, skip to the steps that begin with "Making Herb Cheese Rolls." If you decide to mix your herbs into your cheese, continue with "Mixing in Herbs and Salt."

MIXING IN HERBS AND SALT

Blend the herbs and salt together in a small bowl and set aside.

Place 1-pound plastic cheese molds or cottage cheese containers on a rack or a layer of chopsticks over a draining pan.

Spoon about one-third of the curds into the molds or cottage cheese containers. Add a third of the herbs, followed by more cheese curds. Repeat this process until all the herbs and curds are in the molds or containers. Each should contain about 3 inches of curds.

DRAINING THE CURDS

Allow the cheese to drain for 24 hours. It should be reduced to a depth of 1–1½ inches. Test the cheese with your finger. It should be moist, yet somewhat firm. If you want a drier mixture, allow the curds to drain for another 2–4 hours.

CHILLING AND SERVING

The drained cheese should be solid enough to transfer to a small plate or container for the refrigerator. Chill for 2–4 hours before serving.

MAKING HERB CHEESE ROLLS

Spoon the cheese into the molds or cottage cheese containers and let it drain for 8–12 hours. It should reduce to 2–2½ inches high. Test it with your finger: It should be moist, yet somewhat firm. Transfer it from the mold to a small bowl. Stir in the salt and refrigerate for 1 hour.

In the meantime, in a small bowl blend the three herbs together with a fork. Spread the herbs on a flat surface and remove the cheese from the refrigerator. Spoon the cheese out of the bowl and shape it into a roll with your hands. Then roll the cheese over the herbs until all sides are coated. Wrap in plastic cheese wrap and refrigerate until ready to serve.

LEVEL
Easy, with little processing time

START TO FINISH
1 hour

BEST USE
Table and snack cheese

STORAGE
Keeps well for 5–7 days when refrigerated in an airtight container

YIELD
1–1¼ pounds Finnish cheese

FINNISH LEIPÄJUUSTO

The recipe for this simple and nutritious cheese from Finland was passed along to me by Polly Fafach at Lakehaven Farms. Ideal for snacks, it's a sweet, mild cheese with so much body it "squeaks" when you bite into it. By itself somewhat bland, Leipäjuusto marries well with herbs and spices: Try a teaspoon of fresh lemon zest, caraway, or ground green peppercorns. This cheese also offers a slightly toasted flavor, because it sits under the broiler before you cut it into cubes.

INGREDIENTS

1½ gallons fresh raw goat's milk

¼ teaspoon liquid calf's rennet

¼–½ teaspoon salt, to taste

1–1½ teaspoon seasoning (optional), such as caraway, cracked pepper, and/or lemon zest

HEATING THE MILK

In a double boiler, heat the milk slowly, for about 30 minutes, until it reaches a temperature of 100–105°F.

ADDING THE RENNET

Add ¼ teaspoon liquid calf's rennet and gently blend into the milk with a wire whisk.

RIPENING

Remove the milk pot from the heat, cover with the pot lid, and allow to ripen for 30 minutes in a draft-free area in your kitchen.

DRAINING THE CURDS

Pour the curds into a colander lined with cheesecloth or buttercloth. Lift and tie the edges of the cloth to form a bag. Squeeze out the remaining whey with your hands. When you untie the cloth, the cheese should be a solid yet pliant mass.

ADDING THE SEASONINGS

Add your chosen flavorings. Gently fold into the cheese.

BROILING THE CHEESE

Preheat the broiler. Turn the cheese onto a broiler pan that has slots for drainage. Pat the cheese into a pancake about the size of a dinner plate, and ⅜–½ inch thick.

Broil for 2–3 minutes, or until the top of the cheese forms a golden crust. Remove and set aside to cool for a minute before cutting into bite-size (½-inch) cubes. Serve immediately or store in an airtight container in the refrigerator.

TIP... *Leipäjuusto stands up well when heated in a domed outdoor grill. You'll still need a slotted pan for draining, since the cheese releases additional whey under heat. If you're a stickler for authenticity, Finnish tradition requires the cheese to be charred on a wooden paddle over an open fire.*

CREAM CHEESE

Although the city of Philadelphia has long been synony-
mous with cream cheese, you will be encouraged to hear
you can make it anywhere—and with a number of
variations. Once you've allowed the curds to drain, stir in
your favorite berries, herbs, spices, or even a blue-veined
cheese. Cream cheese mixed with fresh, whole blueber-
ries remains the favorite in our house.

LEVEL
Easy, with little cooking or handwork

START TO FINISH
36–40 hours

BEST USE
Good for the table as a fresh spread, and
also good for baking. This cream cheese
works reliably for homemade cheesecake.

STORAGE
Keeps well for 7–10 days with refrigeration

YIELD
8–10 ounces

TIP... *Start this recipe in the morning for cream cheese the following afternoon. Not much work to do, but a long wait.*

INGREDIENTS

3 cups whole cow's milk

3 cups whipping cream

1/2 teaspoon mesophilic powdered starter

2 drops liquid calf rennet

HEATING THE MILK

Place the milk and whipping cream in a double boiler, and blend together with a wire whisk. Barely heat the milk to 72°F. Remove the milk pot from the stove and place it in a draft-free spot in the kitchen.

ADDING STARTER AND RENNET

Sprinkle the starter on the surface of the milk, and gently stir in a figure-eight pattern to blend. Add the rennet and gently blend it into the mixture. Cover the pot.

RIPENING

Allow the milk mixture to ripen for 24–26 hours. Your goal: a somewhat firm mass that resembles yogurt.

DRAINING THE CURDS

Line a stainless-steel colander with cheesecloth or buttercloth, and place it in a basin to collect the whey. (You can save the whey for baking or for another batch of cheese.) Slowly pour the curds into the colander. Bring up the ends of the cloth, and knot them to form a bag. Support the bag by placing a dowel or chopsticks under the knot, hang the bag over the milk pot, and let the curds drain for another 12 hours, until the whey ceases to run off and you have a solid mass.

BLENDING THE CURDS AND SERVING

Spoon the curds into a bowl or refrigerator container. With a mixing spoon or paddle, blend the curds into a smooth mound of cream cheese. You'll find it hard to resist testing the curds with your index finger, and for many this taste test is critical. To give the flavor a chance to steep, refrigerate for 1 hour before serving.

TIP... *For variety use cow's milk with cream. Or try whole organic chocolate milk. Your product will retain a creamy, tangy texture that is slightly reminiscent of silky mousse, but without the richness. The color of hot chocolate, this marries well with toasted hazelnuts or chestnuts.*

COTTAGE CHEESE

If you gauged only by look and feel, homemade cottage cheese, also known as *pot cheese*, is a twin of the commercial varieties. But the taste! Without the flavor enhancers and preservatives of commercial cheese, you taste nothing but fresh whole milk transformed into nutritious, creamy curds. This is real food, with a tang that sets it off from store brands. If you prefer a milder cottage cheese, rinse the curds in cool water to neutralize the tang (but you'll be missing a rare taste experience). Serve this cheese alone, or sprinkled with ground paprika and parsley.

LEVEL
Easy

START TO FINISH
24 hours (a good cheese to start in late morning or midday)

BEST USE
Good table and cooking cheese

STORAGE
Keeps well for 7–10 days with refrigeration

YIELD
1¼–1½ pounds small-curd cottage cheese

INGREDIENTS

- 1 gallon pasteurized whole cow's milk
- 4 ounces fresh, or ½ teaspoon powdered, mesophilic direct-set starter culture (contains culture and rennet)
- 2–4 tablespoons heavy cream
- ¼ teaspoon fine salt

TIP... *Start this recipe in late morning or midday and finish it the next day. On that day, plan on 45–55 minutes to cook and stir the curds.*

HEATING THE MILK

Slowly heat the milk in a double boiler until the temperature reads between 70° and 72°F.

ADDING THE STARTER

Gently stir the mesophilic starter culture into the warm milk, making sure that it blends evenly. Remove the pot, with the thermometer inside, from the stove. Cover with the pot lid and place the pot in a draft-free spot in your kitchen. The curds set best at 70–72°. If maintaining the temperature is a challenge, wrap a terry towel around the pot for added insulation.

CURDLING TIME

Allow the curds to incubate for 15–20 hours (overnight). Your goal: a firm but not extremely dense consistency.

CUTTING THE CURDS

With a stainless-steel curd knife, gently cut the curds into ⅜- to ½-inch cubes. Allow the curds to settle for 30 minutes. The whey will rise to the top of the mixture.

STIRRING THE CURDS

For the next 45–55 minutes, heat the curds very gradually in their pot in a double boiler, one degree at a time. Each increase in temperature should take 1–1½ minutes. Stir the curds every 5 minutes to prevent them from sticking together, or you will have one mass of curd instead of creamy yet distinct clumps.

Continue to stir, while raising the temperature to 110°F—about 15–20 minutes.

Hold the temperature at 110°F, and stir for 25–35 minutes. You'll see the curds start to firm up, as the remaining whey cooks out. To test firmness, squeeze a piece of curd between your fingers: It should feel solid and inclined to spring back against the pressure. If the curd remains soft or feels mushy, continue to stir, expelling more of the whey.

Once you are satisfied with the texture, take the curd pot out of the double boiler and set it aside for 10 minutes, giving the cheese a chance to settle to the bottom again.

DRAINING THE CURDS

Line a stainless-steel or enamel colander with fine cheesecloth or buttercloth and place it in a basin to collect the whey. Do not place the colander in your sink, unless you have thoroughly scalded the sink first. (You run the risk of exposing the curds to unwanted bacteria, which will contaminate the cheese.)

Slowly pour the curds and whey into the colander and allow the mixture to drain for another 10 minutes. Congratulations. You now have a batch of fresh cottage cheese.

WASHING THE CURDS

Prepare a bowl of cool water to refresh the cheese. Washing the curds will neutralize any excess tang and firm up the curds. Pull up the ends of the cheesecloth or buttercloth so that it looks like a bag, and dip it into the bowl of water two or three times.

Allow the cottage cheese to drain again in a colander while you fill another bowl with ice water. Dip the bag of cottage cheese into the bowl, then transfer it to the colander to drain for 15 minutes.

BLENDING THE CURDS AND SERVING

With a large, sterile, slotted stainless-steel spoon, transfer the cottage cheese from the cloth to a glass mixing bowl. Gently loosen the curds with a fork, just in case some have clung together. Add 2 tablespoons of heavy cream, and gently blend it into the cottage cheese with the fork. If you want a creamier mixture, blend in the remaining two tablespoons of heavy cream.

Sprinkle the salt over the mixture and blend with the fork again. Transfer your cheese to an airtight container and refrigerate for 2 hours before serving.

Cutting the curds

Stirring the curds

Straining the curds

Draining the curds

LEVEL
Easy

START TO FINISH
4–4½ hours

BEST USES
Good for cooking, broiling, and frying

STORAGE
Keeps well for 7–10 days when refrigerated in an airtight container

YIELD
1–1¼ pounds queso blanco

QUESO BLANCO

If you enjoy preparing (and eating) ethnic foods, you're probably familiar with queso blanco (white cheese). Queso fresco is white, crumbly, and moist. Queso chihuahua is a milder, pale yellow cheese, which behaves much like Cheddar for cooking and eating. However, queso blanco remains the queen of cheeses for Mexican cuisine. It and queso fresco have been staples in South American and Mexican cooking for decades. You will find queso blanco relatively simple to make and versatile. A sturdy yet tender cheese with a mild flavor, its texture makes it good for baking, broiling, or frying. The next time you offer guests a Mexican spread, include Queso Blanco Enchiladas (page 125) and stand back for the "Olé!"

INGREDIENTS

1 gallon whole goat's or cow's milk

¼ cup cider vinegar

TIP... *You'll get a delicious queso blanco whether you use goat's or cow's milk. The cheese from goat's milk will be a bit whiter and carry a little more tang.*

HEATING THE MILK

You need no double boiler for this cheese. Heat the milk gradually over medium-low direct heat for 20–30 minutes, or until it reaches a temperature of 175–180°F. It's important to heat gradually, and to stir the milk frequently to prevent scorching (and a slightly burnt taste).

ADDING THE VINEGAR

Hold the temperature at 175–180°F for about 10 minutes—lower the heat, if necessary. (Once milk reaches high temperatures, it can gain heat surprisingly quickly.) Slowly stir in the vinegar, until the milk acidifies and curds form.

DRAINING THE CURDS

Remove the pot from the heat. In a sterile basin, place a colander lined with enough cheesecloth or butter-cloth to tie into a knot. Pour or ladle the curds into the lined colander. (At this point, you can collect the whey for ricotta or any other whey cheese. Just remember that you need to use the whey within 1 hour after collecting it, before it gets cold.)

Tie the corners of the cloth into a knot, forming a bag from which to drain off the whey. Slide two chopsticks or a long-handled spoon beneath the knot and transfer the bag to hang inside the empty milk pot to drain. Set the pot aside and allow the cheese to drain for 3–5 hours or until it stops dripping.

REFRIGERATING AND SERVING

Remove the bag from the pot, untie it, and turn the cheese into a bowl for immediate use or refrigerate it in a plastic container.

TIP... *You can make queso blanco in the afternoon for dinner the same day. Also known as a bag cheese, because of the way it drains, queso blanco is ready to use immediately after you drain the curds.*

WHOLE-CREAM RICOTTA

Practical and delicious, whole-cream ricotta is a favorite for baking. It's just a little moister than whey ricotta (page 56), remains very creamy, and takes on the redolence and flavor of whatever food it marries. This recipe makes great lasagna and manicotti and irresistible Ricotta Pie (see page 130).

LEVEL
Medium (requires a certain amount of unattended cooking)

START TO FINISH
About 1½ hours

BEST USE
Good table and cooking cheese

STORAGE
Keeps well for 4–5 days in the refrigerator

YIELD
About 16 ounces fresh ricotta

INGREDIENTS

½ gallon whole cow's milk

1 cup heavy cream

7 tablespoons fresh lemon juice

¼ teaspoon salt

HEATING THE MILK

Blend the milk, cream, and lemon juice in a saucepan or small milk pot, and place over medium-low heat. Allow the mixture to heat for 45–50 minutes, until the temperature reaches 165–170°F. Stir the milk mixture once or twice during heating, to avoid sticking. If you stir the milk more frequently, the ricotta curds will be smaller than you want them. As the milk heats, it forms into small pea- or lentil-sized curds.

WARMING THE CURDS

Increase the heat slightly closer to medium, and continue to warm the curds for another 7–8 minutes, or until they reach 200–205°F along the sides of the pot as well as in the middle, as measured by your dairy thermometer. Your goal: curds the consistency of a creamy custard, with the liquid on the verge of boiling. Small mounds will form on the surface and begin to spout.

COOLING AND DRAINING THE CURDS

Remove the pot from the heat and allow the ricotta mixture to rest for 15 minutes. The curds will settle to the bottom, and excess whey will continue to rise to the top.

Line a colander with a double thickness of damp cheesecloth or buttercloth. Ladle the curds into the colander and allow them to drain for 20 minutes. The ricotta should be thick and creamy.

ADDING THE SALT AND SERVING

Stir in the salt, and use the ricotta immediately or refrigerate it.

TIP... *You can easily make this recipe in a day, and you may be tempted to double the recipe. Don't. With this uncomplicated recipe, I frequently make two batches of fresh ricotta in the same afternoon. When you are making cheese from scratch, timing and volume play a major role in its success.*

WHEY RICOTTA

Watch this ricotta form right before your eyes! You'll make it with whey saved from other cheese recipes in the book. It's delicious with fruit and herbs and combines well in quiches and omelets. For an elegant dessert that blends ricotta and fromage blanc, try the Fromage Strawberry Wreath on page 133. Or bake a Ricotta Pie (page 130)—you'll never make another cheesecake.

INGREDIENTS

- 2 gallons fresh goat or cow whey
- ¼ cup cider vinegar
- ¼ cup heavy cream (optional)
- Salt to taste

HEATING THE WHEY

Stir the whey directly over medium heat (not in a double boiler) until it reaches 200°F. Then gently stir in the vinegar and remove the pot from the burner. Small pieces of white curd should begin to form and float to the top of the whey.

DRAINING THE WHEY

Carefully pour the hot mixture into a colander lined with a piece of fine cheesecloth or buttercloth. Tie the corners of the cloth and allow the curds to drain for 3–4 hours, until all the remaining whey has dripped off.

ADDING SALT AND SERVING

Lift the knotted cloth out of the colander and turn the curds into a bowl. At this point, you can stir in the cream and a little salt for a moister ricotta mixture. Serve immediately or refrigerate.

TIP...
Avoid disappointment!
- *Buy high-quality milk.*
- *Save the whey from recipes that heat at lower, not higher, temperatures.*
- *Remember to use the whey while it's still warm, within 1½ hours.*

LEVEL
Medium

START TO FINISH
4–5 hours

BEST USE
Good table and cooking cheese

STORAGE
Keeps well in the refrigerator for 5–7 days

YIELD
About 1½ cups fresh ricotta

LEVEL
Medium (working the curd takes a little practice)

START TO FINISH
24 hours, or a day and overnight

BEST USE
Good table, cooking, and melting cheese

STORAGE
Keeps well in the refrigerator for up to 1 week, freezes well for 2–3 months.

YIELD
About 1 pound mozzarella

MOZZARELLA

The milk of many a water buffalo has contributed to the making of a fine mozzarella. Its flavor, texture, and melt-down factors make this milk the favorite for those who can find it and afford it. Where they were plentiful and available, buffalo were milked for this cheese, but dairy farmers and cheese makers throughout Italy and the United States turned to what was available (and it usually wasn't buffalo). Great mozzarella has been produced from cow's, goat's, and even sheep's milk, along with buffalo's. (When you're ready to serve your mozzarella in a taste-tantalizing dish, try Lemon Mozzarella with Parmesan Crostini, page 119.)

TIPS... *If you're a novice cheese maker, I recommend using whole cow's milk, which contains a higher percentage of fat, for your first batch of mozzarella. Fresh goat's milk produces a cheese that can be a bit less pliable. If you use raw milk, be sure to pasteurize it first.*

If you want to save the whey from your mozzarella to make ricotta, plan ahead—you need to use the whey within 1½ hours after you collect it. Whey from a gallon of milk is a good amount for your first test batch of ricotta. I usually collect whey from two gallons when I need a batch for cooking or baking.

INGREDIENTS

1 gallon whole goat's milk or whole cow's milk

1¼ teaspoons citric acid powder, dissolved in 4 tablespoons cold water

¼ rennet tablet

¼ cup cool water

⅓ cup flake salt

Note: You'll need pH strips for testing acidity in this recipe (for sources, see pages 136).

HEATING THE MILK

In a double boiler, heat the pasteurized milk to 90°F. Spoon out a sample of milk for testing acidity. Dip a pH strip into the sample. It should read 6.8pH, which is standard for fresh milk.

ADDING THE CITRIC ACID AND RENNET

With the double boiler still on the stove, add the diluted citric acid and gently blend into the milk with a whisk. Allow the milk to rest for 45 minutes. Crush the rennet into powder with a teaspoon and blend it into ¼ cup cool water. Add the rennet to the milk mixture and blend in. Remove the milk from the stove.

RIPENING

Cover the milk pan with a lid and set aside in a draft-free spot for 1½ hours to ripen. Your goal: When you test the curd with the tip of a sterile knife, it should have the consistency of a thick yogurt.

CUTTING THE CURD

Take your time cutting the curd. With a long curd knife, cut from left to right, top to bottom, then horizontally across the curds on a diagonal to the bottom of the pot, cutting the curd in 1½-inch cubes. Allow the curds to rest for 30 minutes. They will settle to the bottom of the pot and firm up, as the whey rises.

TESTING ACIDITY

Use a pH strip to test for acidity once again. Spoon out a sample of the whey and dip the pH strip into it. The pH paper should read right around 6.5. If it doesn't, let the curd sit awhile longer, then test again.

INCREASING THE HEAT

Return the double boiler to the stove top. Slowly increase the heat of the milk, *by about 2 degrees every five to six minutes*, until the temperature reaches 100°F. (Rapid heating will prevent the curd from coagulating.)

Stir the curds once or twice during the heating period, or just enough to keep them separated as they shrink, as more whey rises to the surface. Once the curds have reached 100°F, remove the double boiler from the heat and allow the curds to settle for 10 minutes.

TIP... *Expect to make mozzarella more than once or twice before you're comfortable with the final product. An acquired skill, it involves techniques of heating, cooling, working the curds, and stretching that improve with practice. But believe me, even your first attempts—no matter what they look like—will taste good.*

DRAINING THE CURDS

Remove the pot of curds from the stove and place it in a basin or sink of slightly warm water (100°F) to acidify further. The whey will continue to rise to the top of the curds—drain it off or remove it with a ladle after 30 minutes. Then flip the mass of curds over.

Repeat this ladling and flipping process four more times—a total of five times over a 2½-hour period. (This is the kind of process that separates the dedicated and patient cheese maker from the dabbler.)

Once again, spoon up a bit of whey and test for acidity with a pH strip. At this point, the reading should be 5.3. If not, keep the curds in the warm water bath until the acid level reaches 5.3.

WORKING THE CURDS

Heat ½ gallon of water to about 170°F and blend in the flake salt as you maintain that temperature. Keep the saline solution at 170°F while you are cutting the curds. Take care not to exceed this temperature.

Turn the curds onto a sterile cutting board or work surface. With the curd knife, make slices about ½ inch thick, and then cut the slices into cubes that measure ½–¾ inches. Place the curd cubes in a basin and cover them with the hot saltwater.

Use two wooden spoons to work the curds in the basin (flat-sided spoons work best) and press them together. Continue to use the spoons to encourage the curds to form a smooth mass, with no cubelike shapes. This process may take about 20 minutes, and the result will be a smooth, shiny, pliant ball of fresh mozzarella.

This ball should be easy to pull and stretch, like a batch of saltwater taffy. Gently pull at an end of it, to check its resilience. Continue working the curds with the wooden spoons until the water gets cloudy and small surface blisters begin to form on the cheese.

Note: If you are making stuffed or braided mozzarella (see pages 60 and 62), add the filling or braid the cheese at this point.

COOLING THE FORMED MOZZARELLA

Transfer the mozzarella to a bowl of cool water to refresh and firm it. Allow the cheese to rest in the cool water for 10 minutes, then transfer it to a solution of ½ gallon of cool water blended with 2 cups of salt. (You will know you have enough salt in the water when salt residue lies at the bottom of the bowl.)

Cover the bowl of cheese in the salt solution with a kitchen towel and allow it to sit for 8–12 hours, or overnight.

REFRIGERATING AND SERVING

Remove your fresh mozzarella from the saltwater and serve immediately, or refrigerate. Fresh mozzarella keeps best when stored in cheesewrap or an airtight container. Like your other handmade, preservative-free cheeses, plan to use fresh mozzarella within a week or so, or freeze it for 2–3 months.

Mozzarella fresh from the saltwater, ready to serve

STUFFED MOZZARELLA

Once you've met the challenge of creating a pliant ball of mozzarella, you can delight friends with variations on it—stuffed or braided cheese, or smoked mozzarella, also known as scamorze. I am including three of my family's favorite stuffed mozzarellas, and you're sure to come up with creative combinations of your own.

INGREDIENTS

For 1 pound of mozzarella, use a filling that measures ¾–1 cup.

CHOOSE FROM:

¾ cup mascarpone blended with 1 tablespoon fresh grated lemon zest;

OR

¾ cup ricotta blended with 2 tablespoons sliced green olive;

OR

¾ cup softened homemade cream cheese blended with 2 tablespoons smoked salmon

STUFFING

Prepare to stuff mozzarella after you've finished working the curds, and before cooling or refreshing the cheese in a basin of water. Remove the newly worked mozzarella ball from the warm water. Place it on a flat surface and stretch the ball from the center. Work quickly to shape it into a disk no thicker than 3/8 inch. Place the filling in the center of the cheese, and fold the ends from top to bottom and from side to side, smoothing out the seams. Be sure that all ends of the mozzarella are completely sealed.

COOLING AND SERVING

Following the instructions for plain mozzarella (page 59), transfer the stuffed mozzarella to the basin of cool water and allow it to rest immersed for about 10 minutes. Then move the mozzarella to the salt brine solution and allow it to soak for 1 hour before serving or refrigerating.

LEVEL
Medium

START TO FINISH
24 hours to make the mozzarella

BEST USE
Good table, cooking, and melting cheese

STORAGE
Keeps well in the refrigerator for up to 1 week, freezes well for 2–3 months.

YIELD
About 1 pound

California Buffalo

Lovers of mozzarella know that the real thing comes only from the milk of the water buffalo—*mozzarella di bufala*. And some of the most acclaimed buffalo mozzarella—at least in the western United States—is made at Virgilio Ciccione's Italcheese company in Southern California.

In 1983, native Italians Virgilio and his brother Jerry decided to switch from making their living as California swordfishermen to making their living as California cheese makers. They bought equipment, cultures, and rennet and hired a staff to work the cultures, heat the milk, and knead, stretch, and ripen the cheese. But the cheese didn't stretch. One cheese factory and $36,000 later, still no cheese.

"I called the people to come out and start breaking up the factory, this factory that never was a factory," Virgilio told the *Los Angeles Times* in March 1998. "That's when my wife called and said, 'You know that cheese you brought over last weekend? I was doing some pasta for the kids, so I put a little of the cheese in hot water like I saw you do, and it stretched. I made it into a little ball and put a little salt on it and ate it. It was good.'" The problem proved to have been the antibiotics in U.S. milk, which killed off much of the bacterial culture essential to the mozzarella-making process.

What's so great about *mozzarella di bufala*? "You cannot compare this cheese with anything else," Ciccione says. "You eat it and it melts in your mouth." Some people don't like the rich, earthy, yogurtlike flavor, among them Ciccione's wife. "But she also hates caviar and truffles," Ciccione explains.

If you're eager to try your hand at buffalo mozzarella, you need to know that only about 3,500 water buffaloes live in the United States—Ciccione gets his from the B&B Ranch near Fresno, California, and the Turkey Creek Company in Texarkana, Arkansas. You could start there.

BRAIDED MOZZARELLA

Braided mozzarella takes just one more step than plain mozzarella. The result is an impressive, thick braid of cheese.

LEVEL
   Medium

START TO FINISH
   24 hours to make the mozzarella
   15–20 minutes for braiding

BEST USE
   Good table, cooking, and melting cheese

STORAGE
   Keeps well in the refrigerator for up to 1 week; freezes well for 2–3 months

YIELD
   About 1 pound braided mozzarella

To prepare mozzarella for shaping, the curds are slowly molded in warm water.

As a solid, elastic mass, the curds are rolled into a rope…

BRAIDING

Follow the steps for plain mozzarella, but after working the curds and before cooling the cheese, remove the worked mozzarella ball from the warm water.

Working quickly (mozzarella loses its flexibility as it cools), stretch the ball into a rope. Then, starting at the center, cross one half of the rope over the other to begin the braid. Continue to cross over with one end, then the other, until the rope is completely braided.

COOLING AND SERVING

The mozzarella is now ready for cooling and soaking in the salt solution. Proceed as for plain mozzarella, page 59.

Then braided or twisted into the desired shape.

SCAMORZE

Scamorze is the label that incredibly in-the-know cheese lovers give to mozzarella or other varieties of semisoft cheese that have been smoked. In the photo, scamorze is contrasted to a ball of fresh white mozzarella.

LEVEL
Medium

START TO FINISH
24 hours to make the mozzarella
6–9 hours for preparation and smoking

BEST USE
Good table, cooking, and melting cheese

STORAGE
Keeps well in the refrigerator for up to 1 week; freezes well for 2–3 months.

YIELD
About 1 pound scamorze

INGREDIENTS AND EQUIPMENT

Smoker, or kettle grill plus an indirect source of low heat and a pan of water

Smoking material—dampened grass, ground nutshells, wood or apple chips, or your own creation

Ball of mozzarella

Cheesecloth or buttercloth

Mesh screen

TIP... *Whether you choose to use a grill or a smoker can dramatically affect how you smoke cheese. The most important factor is still the need to "smoke" or flavor the cheese, not cook it. If you use a grill or a one-chamber smoker, use only 4–5 pieces of charcoal, wood, or other heating material.*

SMOKING

If you use a kettle grill, place the dampened smoking materials into an aluminum pan and put the pan in the coals. If you use a regular smoker, follow the instructions that you would use for any other food, making sure that the heat doesn't get too intense—or you may end up with cheese soup.

Wrap the mozzarella in cheesecloth or buttercloth and place it on a mesh screen, which in turn rests on the upper rack of the grill or smoker. Smoke the mozzarella for 5–8 hours, or until the outside is golden brown.

COOLING AND SERVING

Remove the smoked cheese from the unit and allow it to cool completely before serving.

WEINKASE

When you combine a moderately sweet white wine, herbs, and cheese, you create *weinkase* (wine cheese), a unique table cheese that increases in flavor as it steeps. Its name recognizes Germany's achievements in the making of fine wine, as well as fine cheese. This recipe adds a touch of romance to the craft, and you'll find it's worth the effort, particularly for special occasions and holidays.

LEVEL
Medium (careful handwork needed when draining and pressing the cheese)

START TO FINISH
1 hour to form and drain the curds

24 hours to press the curds

24 hours to soak the pressed cheese

3–4 weeks to age before serving (optional, but the longer you wait, the better it tastes)

BEST USE
Table cheese

STORAGE
Keeps in the refrigerator for about 7–10 days after it's been cut

YIELD
12–14 ounces white wine cheese

INGREDIENTS

2 gallons fresh whey from cow's milk

2 cups whole milk

2 cups light cream

¼ cup tarragon vinegar

2 cups white medium-dry wine

2 cups water

2 tablespoons coarse salt

¼ cup fresh tarragon

TIP... *The techniques of aging, or adding butter, wine, and herbs to fresh and aged cheese, have refined a very technical process to an art. Aging adds the maturity and resonance that characterize memorable cheeses. Like fine old wines, mature cheeses have a depth and body not found in young, fresh cheeses.*

HEATING THE MILK

In a large saucepan or stockpot, stir the whey, milk, and light cream with a whisk, until all of the ingredients are well mixed. Place the pot directly over medium-low heat and warm the liquid for approximately 20 minutes, or until it reaches 180°F.

FORMING THE CURDS

Gently stir the milk blend as you add the tarragon vinegar. Remove the pot from the heat and set it aside to rest for 15–20 minutes, as small curds float to the surface.

DRAINING THE CURDS

Pour the curds and whey into a colander lined with a double thickness of moist cheesecloth or buttercloth large enough to tie over the mixture. Tie the corners of the cloth to form a bag, run a dowel or chopsticks under the knot, and hang the cheese over the stockpot for 5 hours, until well drained.

PRESSING THE CURDS

Line the canister of the cheese press with a double thickness of cheesecloth or buttercloth. Turn the curds into the canister, add the followers, and press the cheese at 15 pounds of pressure for 12–15 hours.

BRINING THE CHEESE

Release the pressure clamp, take the cheese from the canister, and unwrap it. Pour the white wine, water, and salt into a basin or bowl and blend with a wire whisk. Add the tarragon and the cheese. Seal the bowl with plastic wrap and place it in the refrigerator for 24 hours.

SERVING

Remove the bowl and take the cheese out of the liquid. At this point, you can serve the cheese or age it to an even more delectable flavor for 3–4 weeks in the refrigerator.

Spoon curds gently into the cheese-press cylinder lined with cheese-cloth, with a basin or shallow bowl standing by to collect additional whey.

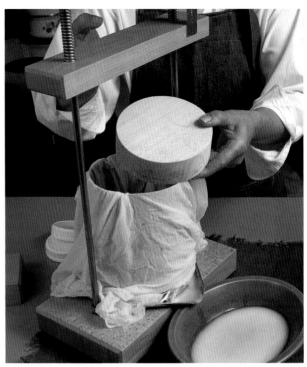

Pieces of hardwood, called followers, follow the curds into the cylinder to maintain tension and balance during the pressing process.

Followers are added until the pressing surface sits above the rim of the cylinder, to give the pressure bar something to press down on.

mold- and age-ripened cheeses

STILTON

One of the loftiest of blue-mold cheeses, Stilton originated in Leicestershire and parts of Nottinghamshire, England, and today graces tables around the globe. This British cheese combines the flavor and smooth texture of Cheddar with the musty spice of a softer, blue-veined cheese. I have found this Stilton recipe a little less tricky than those for other blues. Most commercial varieties arrive as wheels weighing up to 16 pounds, dwarfing your handmade round. Yet you'll match the flavor of your homemade Stilton against any store brand. This cheese enhances the flavor of sweeter fruits and partners well with milder vegetables, greens, and bread.

LEVEL

Medium (requires handwork, patience, and time)

START TO FINISH

About 5 hours for heating and ripening

About 2 hours for molding

2–15 hours (or overnight) for setting

3 days for draining

3 months for curing

BEST USE

Good table cheese

STORAGE

Several weeks, when well sealed in the refrigerator

YIELD

About 1 1/2–2 pounds Stilton

TIP... *I never cease to be amazed at how slight, seemingly negligible changes in timing, stirring, washing, or settling, can produce cheese vastly different in flavor, flower, and feel.*

This blue takes a bit of time, and like others of its class requires plenty of aging time. Try making it in late spring, for a special touch at Christmas.

INGREDIENTS

2 gallons whole cow's milk

2 1/2 cups heavy cream

1/2 teaspoon powdered mesophilic starter

2–3 tablespoons flake salt

1/4 teaspoon blue-mold powder

2 teaspoons liquid rennet in 1/4 cup cool water

HEATING AND ADDING CULTURE

In a double boiler, blend the milk and the cream, and warm to 88°F. Gently stir in the starter culture, turn off the heat under the pot, and allow the milk to ripen for 45 minutes.

ADDING RENNET AND COOKING AND CUTTING THE CURDS

Add the liquid rennet to 1/4 cup cool water and gently stir the liquid into the cultured milk, using a wire whisk to make sure that all of the ingredients are blended. Do not stir the milk vigorously. Cover the pot and allow the milk to ripen for 1 1/2–2 hours, or until the curds make a clean break when cut with a curd knife (no curds cling to the knife).

Cut the curds into 1/2-inch cubes and allow them to rest for 20 minutes, as the whey rises to the surface.

DRAINING AND PRESSING THE CURDS

Line a colander with a double thickness of fine cheesecloth or buttercloth large enough to tie into a knot to make a bag to hold the curds. Place the colander in a sterile basin. Use a large slotted spoon to transfer the curds to the colander; then allow the curds to rest for an hour.

Tie the corners of the cloth together to form a bag, and slide a dowel or chopsticks under the knot. Hang the bag inside the milk pot, held up by the dowel, and allow the curds to continue to drain for another 30–45 minutes, or until the whey ceases to drip.

Transfer the bag of curds to a cheese press or a shallow bowl. Top the curds with a board, if you are pressing by hand, then a 5-pound weight. If you are using a press, top with a follower and apply 5 pounds of pressure. Allow the cheese to rest 12–15 hours, or overnight, in a draft-free area of the kitchen.

MILLING AND SALTING THE CURDS

Release the press or board, take the curds out of the cloth as a solid mass, and transfer to a large bowl or sterile basin. Use the curd knife to cut the curds into 1- to 1½-inch cubes. In a small bowl or measuring cup, blend 2 tablespoons salt with ¼ teaspoon blue-mold powder. Sprinkle the mixture over the curds and blend all of the ingredients together with a slotted spoon, or your hands, until all the curds are coated with the salt and powder.

MOLDING AND DRAINING THE CHEESE

Plan on 3 days to mold and drain the Stilton. Place a cheese board in a shallow draining pan. Top the board with a cheese mat, followed by a 2-pound mold. Ladle the curds into the mold, and cover it with another mat and board or saucer.

Allow the cheese to drain for 1½ hours, turning it every 30 minutes—3 times in all. Then let the cheese set for 12–15 hours or overnight. Let it continue to drain for the next 3 days, turning the mold every 8–12 hours. Your cheese is now ready for aging.

Piercing a Stilton through and through before applying blue-mold powder *(penicillium roqueforti)* to induce the blue striations of veined cheeses.

AGING THE CHEESE

Remove the cheese from the mold and pierce it from one flat side through the other with a sterile ice pick. Remove the pick and place the pierced cheese on a flat plate or rack that is topped with a mat. Place the cheese in a cool room or a refrigerator where the climate can be controlled. You need to age this cheese at 50°F and at 85 percent humidity.

Once a week, gently scrape away any heavy surface mold or slime with a butter knife. (Air circulation is critical to the forming of the blue veins inside the cheese and on the surface.)

Age your Stilton for at least 90 days before you taste it; it will be full of flavor, yet somewhat mild. If you prefer a stronger cheese, let it continue to age, testing and tasting it every 30 days, up to 6 months.

LEVEL
    Medium

START TO FINISH
    About 15 hours,
    plus aging time

BEST USE
    Good table and
    cooking cheese

STORAGE
    An aged cheese
    that keeps well in
    the meat or
    vegetable section
    of your refrigera-
    tor. Tightly
    wrapped or
    sealed in a plastic
    container, it stays
    fresh for 10 days
    to 2 weeks.

YIELD
    1½–2 pounds
    American brick

ALL-AMERICAN BRICK

This historic cheese first appeared on the tables of seventeenth-century colonists along the North American shores of the Atlantic. Its creamy texture and tangy flavor make it a popular partner for a variety of breads, soups, and desserts. Try it grilled with sliced tomatoes on sourdough, blend a little into your potato soup, or serve it with nutmeg over warm apple pie.

TIP... *Making this cheese takes some practice, and I recommend you try it only after you've gained some experience with heating, renneting, washing, and salting. Brick is a time-consuming cheese to cook, and it requires patience during the aging process.*

INGREDIENTS

2 gallons whole cow's milk

4 tablespoons fresh, or ½ teaspoon powdered, mesophilic starter

1 drop cheese coloring

¾ teaspoon liquid calf's rennet in ¼ cup cool water

Brine solution: 4 cups salt for 1 gallon water

Bacterial linens powder: 1 teaspoon diluted in 1 quart water

Saline solution for washing cheese: 1 cup salt for 2 quarts water

Brick of red cheese wax, 8 ounces or more (unused wax can be stored)

HEATING THE MILK

Warm two gallons of whole cow's milk in a double boiler over medium-low heat for 15–20 minutes, or until the milk reaches 85–86°F.

ADDING THE STARTER CULTURE

Add the mesophilic starter, and gently but thoroughly blend it into the milk with a wire whisk. Remove the double boiler from the heat, cover, and set aside, to allow the milk to ripen for 20 minutes.

ADDING COLOR

If you prefer a slight buttery yellow hue to this cheese, add one drop of cheese coloring and blend it into the milk mixture at this point. Without the coloring, the cheese will remain white.

ADDING THE RENNET

Dissolve the liquid rennet in ¼ cup cool water. With a whisk, gently stir the rennet solution into the ripened milk, cover, and allow the mixture to set for 30–45 minutes, or when the curd makes a clean break when tested with a knife. The knife should come out easily, with little or no curd clinging to it. If it doesn't, the curds need to set a little longer to solidify.

CUTTING AND COOKING THE CURDS

Cut the curd into ½-inch cubes and return the double boiler to the burner. Cook and slowly stir the curds over medium-low heat to maintain the 85–86°F temperature.

Barely increase the heat under the cooking curds, *1 degree every 5–6 minutes,* so that the temperature in the pot reaches 92°F over a period of 20–30 minutes. Remove the double boiler from the heat and allow the curds to rest for 15 minutes. Cooking shrinks the curds, allowing them to settle as more whey rises to the surface.

DRAINING AND WASHING THE CURDS

While the curds rest, warm 10–12 cups of water, maintaining a temperature of 92°F.

You are now ready to drain the curds of whey and replace the whey with water of the same temperature. Water that is hotter or colder than the existing 92°F can cause a breakdown in the process of coagulation.

Drain the curds with a shallow ladle or large cooking spoon, a cup at a time, until most of the whey has been removed from the surface. Measure the whey as you collect it, because you will replace it with an equal amount of water. (The amount of whey can vary somewhat from one batch of milk to the next.)

You will probably release 10–12 cups of whey, which need to be replaced with 10–12 cups of the warm water. Add the water, then stir the curds for 20–30 minutes, maintaining the temperature of 92˚F.

Remove the double boiler from the heat and set it aside to rest the curds for 15 minutes.

MOLDING AND PRESSING THE CHEESE

Pour or ladle the curds into a 2-pound mold lined with cheesecloth or buttercloth. Cover the curds with the cheesecloth or buttercloth and add 1 or 2 followers. Press under 5 pounds of pressure in a cheese press for 15 minutes. Remove the cheese from the press by hand, flip it over, and return it to the mold . Add the followers and press the cheese again at 5 pounds of pressure for 15 minutes. Continue to press the cheese for the next 8 hours, *turning it once every hour.*

BRINING THE CHEESE

Take the cheese from the press and remove the cloth bandage. The outer surface of the cheese should be smooth and free from any small cracks or splits, which can show up when a cheese has been pressed too dry.

Mix the brine solution in a large bowl or basin and immerse the cheese round in the brine. Allow it to soak for 4–6 hours. Remove the cheese, dry it with a lint-free kitchen towel, and set it aside on a cheese mat or draining rack.

Bacterial linens powder, blended with water in a sterile 1-quart spray bottle and sprayed on some cheeses during the aging process, creates a linenlike effect as mold grows.

ADDING THE BACTERIAL LINENS

Pour 1 quart of cool water into a sterile atomizer and add 1 teaspoon of bacterial linens powder. Shake the atomizer until the mixture is well blended.

Spray all surfaces of the newly pressed cheese with the linens. Return the cheese to the mat and store it, *uncovered,* in a refrigerator or cool room at 58–60˚F and at a humidity of 90 percent for 2 weeks. Use your hands to wash the cheese daily with the saline solution—this keeps the outer surface of the cheese moist and maintains the balance that encourages the red bacteria to develop.

WAXING AND AGING THE CHEESE

You should begin to see signs of red bacteria mold after 10–14 days. Pat the surface of the cheese to remove any excess moisture. Heat a brick of cheese wax until it reaches a liquid state. Brush the wax on all sides of the cheese, making sure that it is completely sealed. (Gaps will promote unwanted bacteria growth and can ruin your efforts.) Store the cheese in the refrigerator or a controlled environment at 45-50˚F for 6 weeks. *Turn the cheese every other day,* to ensure even moisture flow.

DANISH BLUE

Making any blue-veined cheese poses a challenge. The temperamental nature of liquid Roquefort culture along with the requirement that the cheese maker replicate cavelike conditions sends some cooks straight out of the kitchen to the cheese store. Still, with practice you will create fresh Danish blue with a pale creamy interior and a delicate yet somewhat firm texture—a cheese equally delicious on its own or as a "bet you can't eat just one" combination with breads and crackers.

LEVEL
    Fairly difficult

START TO FINISH
    8 hours for the initial heating and ripening
    12 hours for draining (overnight)
    10 days for ripening and curing
    6 months for aging

BEST USE
    Good table cheese

STORAGE
    2–3 months when wrapped and refrigerated

YIELD
    1½ pounds blue cheese

INGREDIENTS

2 gallons whole pasteurized cow's milk

4 ounces mesophilic starter culture

¼ teaspoon liquid *penicillium roqueforti*

1 teaspoon liquid calf's rennet in ¼ cup cool water

2 tablespoons coarse flake salt

HEATING, CULTURING, AND INOCULATING THE MILK

In a double boiler, warm the cow's milk to 90°F. Blend the mesophilic starter into the milk. Add the *penicillium roqueforti* and blend it into the milk mixture. Keep the milk warm enough to maintain 90°F without overheating. Cover the pot and allow the milk to ripen for 1 hour 15 minutes.

ADDING THE RENNET

Blend the liquid rennet with ¼ cup cool water and add the mixture to the milk, still maintaining 90°F. Gently stir with a whisk, cover, and allow to set at 90ºF for 1 hour, or until the formed curds make a clean break when tested with a knife.

COOKING, DRAINING, AND SALTING THE CURDS

Once the curds are set, keep them at 90°F and stir every 5–7 minutes for 1 hour until the curds have shrunk and firmed up and the whey has separated to the surface. Be careful not to stir the curds too frequently or too vigorously.

Let the cooked curds rest for 10 minutes, then slowly pour off the whey. (You probably don't want to save this whey, because of its inoculation.) Pour the curds into a colander lined with cheesecloth or buttercloth and allow them to drain for another 5 minutes. Ladle or pour the curds back into the pot and work them gently with your hand, just enough to prevent them from matting together.

Sprinkle the coarse salt over the curds and gently blend everything with a spoon.

MOLDING AND SALTING THE CHEESE

This process requires 2 hours of handwork—not difficult, but time consuming.

Place a cheese board in a drain pan, and put a cheese mat on top of the board. Put a 2-pound cheese mold on the mat and slowly ladle the salted curds into the mold. Cover the mold with another cheese mat, topped with a board or saucer. This will enable you to keep everything balanced, because the mold needs to be turned every 30 minutes—4 times— in the next 2 hours.

After you have turned the mold for the last time, allow the cheese to drain on its board in the drain pan overnight in a draft-free area of your kitchen.

SALTING AND CHILLING THE CHEESE

Remove the drained cheese from the mold and gently rub a little coarse salt onto all surfaces. Place the cheese on a cheese mat on a flat rack or plate and chill in a cool room or refrigerator at 55–60°F, and a humidity of 85 percent. Allow the cheese to rest in this climate for 3 days, turning and sprinkling the cheese with salt once a day. Dust off any excess salt.

CURING THE CHEESE

Your basement, a small refrigerator, or a refrigerator vegetable bin can become a curing room. I use a bin with a control dial and a hydrometer to read the temperature and humidity.

With a sterile ice pick, pierce the cheese completely through from top to bottom. (This hole will help distribute air, which helps the blue mold form.) Remove the pick and cure the cheese in an environment of 55°F and 90 percent humidity, keeping these conditions constant for 10 days. If the humidity begins to decrease, place a small bowl of warm water beside the cheese.

Since the cheese is moist and a bit soft on the surface, turn it from one flat side to the other every 3 days. This will allow it to maintain a uniform shape while curing.

Blue mold should appear at 10 days. If it doesn't, keep the climate constant and continue to turn the cheese. Since the development of mold is sensitive to many influences, don't be alarmed if it doesn't appear on exactly day 10. Once the mold begins to show, allow it to grow for about 30 days or until the surface of the cheese is covered.

Allow the cheese to cure for another 90 days. During this time, use a sterile butter knife to gently scrape the heavier coat of mold and any slime from the surface of the cheese. (It's important to keep air circulating around and through the cheese, as mold develops not only on the outside, but also on the inside. If the surface of the cheese gets too dense with bacteria matter, it can slow or interrupt air circulation, and consequently the curing process.)

AGING THE CHEESE

After curing, the cheese is ready for 3–6 months of aging. Wrap the blue-veined cheese in plastic cheese wrap and keep it cold, at a temperature of 35°F. Turn it once every 7–10 days. Three months of aging will produce a creamy, mild blue cheese. At 6 months, the cheese will be a little firmer and stronger in flavor.

THANKS...
The general guidelines for this cheese have been generously shared with me by Jim Mildbrand of the Wisby Corporation, a Danish German company with a well-deserved reputation for outstanding cheese cultures and reliable production. Working with Wisby has bolstered my confidence as a cheese maker, particularly a maker of great Danish blue.

CAMEMBERT

One of the finest mold-ripened table cheeses, Camembert repays the careful technique and patience it requires of you. Unlike its pressed cousins, this cheese gains its shape as whey filters through the holes of the container that retains the curds. This somewhat fragile yet full-flavored cheese offers a compelling blend of woody, nutty discoveries for the palate and ripens in just one or two months. Consumed with or without its rind, Camembert adds a special touch to any meal. The cheese marries well with nuts and a variety of fruits, as the Camembert Phyllo recipe on page 111 so deliciously demonstrates.

TIP... Don't make this your first cheese-making project. Camembert isn't a difficult cheese to ripen or cook, but drying, curing, and aging techniques nearly always challenge the novice. If the climate for this cheese is too dry or too cool, the Camembert hardens and dies. If things get a bit too warm and wet, your cheese could sprout growth that rivals any rain forest. Don't be discouraged. Just take some time to understand and study the process and science of mold-ripened cheese. Then it's...Camembert, here you come.

LEVEL
Difficult

START TO FINISH
9–10 hours, or all day, before aging

AGING
6 weeks

BEST USE
Table cheese

STORAGE
5–7 days under refrigeration

YIELD
1½–2 pounds Camembert

INGREDIENTS

2 gallons pasteurized whole goat's milk

½ cup mesophilic starter culture

¼ teaspoon liquid rennet dissolved in ¼ cup cool water

Flake salt or coarse cheese salt

Penicillium candidium powder blended with 1 quart water

Note: For this recipe, you'll need 3 or 4 Camembert cheese cylinders (about 8 ounces each), 4 cheese mats, draining boards and pans, and cheese wrap.

TIP... Camembert calls for special molds that allow drained unbroken curds to be ladled from the vat. This accounts for Camembert's dense, creamy texture. Camembert molds are available from most vendors of cheese supplies.

HEATING AND RIPENING THE MILK

Warm 2 gallons of fresh pasteurized goat's milk in a double boiler for 20 minutes over medium-low heat, until the temperature of the milk reaches 88–90°F. Blend the mesophilic starter culture into the milk. Cover the double boiler, remove it from the heat, and allow the mixture to ripen for 2 hours.

ADDING THE RENNET

Dissolve ¼ teaspoon liquid rennet in ¼ cup cool water and blend the liquid slowly and thoroughly into the ripened milk. Cover the double boiler once again and allow the renneted milk to rest for 1 hour, or until the curd knife makes a clean break, sliding out with no curd clinging to it.

CUTTING AND STIRRING THE CURDS

Maintaining a temperature of 90°F, gently stir the curds for 20–25 minutes. The curds will gradually shrink as the whey rises to the surface. Set the pot of curds aside to rest for 20 minutes.

DRAINING AND MOLDING THE CURDS

Be sure that your molds, cheese mats, and draining boards and pans are completely sterile. Place the boards in the draining pans, place the cheese mats on the boards, and place the Camembert molds on the mats.

Gently ladle the drained curds into the molds, distributing the contents until the molds are nearly full. On top of each mold, place a mat, then a saucer or small cheese board.

TIP... The equipment I use for draining square Camembert includes 8x8 pans or 9x12 pans, with boards that can fit inside them. You can use cutting boards or vegetable boards at least ½ inch high—this allows the whey to run off into the draining pan. To drain round Camembert, I place the molds on chopsticks or some other raised platforms over a square or oblong pan.

You will need to drain the curds and then flip the molds. The mats and saucers or boards will help you balance the molds as you turn them over, as well as keep the curds from spilling out. Drain the curds for an hour, then flip the molds. Repeat this draining and flipping every hour for 6 hours (6 times altogether). The cheese will shrink from about 4 inches to 1½–1¾ inches high and will also shrink away from the sides of the molds.

APPLYING THE WHITE MOLD SPORES

Lift the cheese molds off the cheeses. Sprinkle all sides of each released cheese with salt and set aside on a cheese mat for 15–20 minutes. Pour 1 quart of water into a sterile atomizer, and add a packet of powdered mold. Shake the atomizer to blend the mixture thoroughly, then cover the surface of each cheese with a light spray of the solution.

TIP... *Flake or coarse salt plays a key role in drying and flavoring cheese. The large flecks impregnate the wet curds and encourage evaporation of the excess whey in a manner that smaller granules can't. The same result would require two or three times as much ordinary salt, and you then risk cheese too salty to eat.*

To cure, place the cheeses on mats in an environment that retains a constant temperature of 45°F and humidity of 95 percent. For a curing room, you can use a basement, a small refrigerator, or a refrigerator vegetable bin. I use a refrigerator vegetable bin with a control dial and test the environment with a hygrometer, which reads temperature as well as humidity. This instrument allows me to continually assess the conditions so necessary for the mold to develop.

Allow the cheeses to rest for 5–6 days and check them each day for climate reading and mold development. Once the white mold whiskers begin to appear, gently turn the cheeses over and allow them to continue to develop mold for another 9–10 days.

At this point, white mold should completely cover each cheese—top, bottom, and sides. Wrap the cheeses in cheesewrap specifically developed for the storage of soft cheese. (Although this wrap looks like cellophane, unlike cellophane, it protects the cheese while allowing it to continue to breathe as it ages.) Store the cheeses at 45°F for 4 weeks.

TIP... *Like other mold-ripened cheeses, Camembert requires exact conditions of temperature and humidity. Be sure to store this cheese in a place where you can control these conditions.*

CUTTING AND SERVING

Remove the cheeses from storage, unwrap them, and let them sit at room temperature for 15–20 minutes before cutting. At that point, the top, side walls, and foot of each Camembert should be fairly firm, and the cheese within should be very soft. Serve and enjoy.

age-ripened hard cheeses

MUENSTER

The beauty of this recipe, for me, lies in its simplicity. From just one gallon of goat's or cow's milk, a little rennet, and a bit of salt, you produce a pressed cheese ready for the table after only a week of curing. One of the most versatile of cheeses, Muenster is delicious by itself, cooks and grates nicely, and stores well for weeks. Try it grilled in a sandwich with slices of canned pineapple, bake it, use it to top a pear tart, or fold it into your favorite quesadilla filling.

LEVEL
Fairly easy (an afternoon of processing, a day in the cheese press)

START TO FINISH
60–80 minutes for heating and renneting

20–30 minutes for salting and cooking the curds

20 minutes for draining the curds

24 hours for pressing

5–7 days for curing

BEST USES
Good table and cooking cheese

STORAGE
Tightly wrapped in the refrigerator, stays fresh 10–14 days

YIELD
About 1 pound Muenster

INGREDIENTS

1 gallon whole goat's milk

¼ teaspoon rennet blended with ¼ cup cool water

2 teaspoons fine sea salt

HEATING AND RENNETING THE MILK

Warm the milk for 15–20 minutes in a double boiler, until its temperature reaches 88°F. Remove the pot from the burner and allow it to sit for 5 minutes.

Blend the liquid rennet into the cool water and add this mixture to the milk. Use a whisk to evenly distribute the rennet throughout the mixture, cover the pot, and allow the ingredients to work for 1 hour, or until the whey has risen to the surface and the curd makes a clean break when tested with a knife.

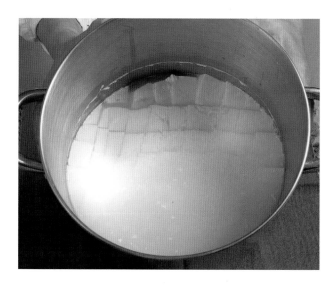

CUTTING THE CURDS, SALTING, AND COOKING

Cut the curd into 1-inch cubes and sprinkle them with the salt. Transfer the double boiler back to the heat and work the salt into the curds with your hands or a large slotted spoon. Be sure to keep low heat under the curds and try to turn, rather than stir, them. (Rapid or vigorous stirring will have a disappointing effect on the flavor and texture of your Muenster.)

DRAINING AND PRESSING THE CURDS

Push the curds into a ball and transfer them to a colander lined with cheesecloth or buttercloth. Let the Muenster drain for 20 minutes.

Once all the whey has been expelled from the cheese, ladle the curds into a 1-pound cheese-press mold lined with cheesecloth or buttercloth. Apply 40 pounds of pressure for 12 hours. Then remove the Muenster, flip it over, rewrap it, and return it to the press. Again apply 40 pounds of pressure for another 12 hours. You now have a 1-pound round of Muenster.

CURING THE CHEESE

Rub your round of Muenster with a little salt, place it on a mat or flat rack, and cover it with a plate (to prevent drying from the top).

The fresh Muenster will take about 5–7 days to form its own rind. Check it, salt it on all sides, and turn it daily. You will see and feel the difference in the surface of the cheese as the outside firms up. Once the rind has formed, your cheese is ready for the table. If you prefer a Muenster with more intense flavor, allow it to steep a week or even a month longer.

TIP... *Make this Muenster with 1 gallon of milk, or double the whole batch. We prefer the flavor that comes with a 1-pound round.*

FETA

Feta has traditionally been produced from sheep's as well as goat's milk. Most Balkan countries make sheep's milk into a rich, bright white, somewhat sweet cheese, but sheep don't give nearly as much milk as goats do, and in many areas their milk is next to impossible to track down. So this recipe calls for goat's milk, and with it you'll make a full pound of Feta—plenty for salads and snacks, with enough left over for cooking and baking. A tasty and elegant example is Feta Spinach Olive Pie (page 121).

LEVEL
Fairly easy
(only a few steps)

START TO FINISH
1¼ hours for heating and ripening

1 hour for renneting and coagulation

50 minutes for curing and stirring the curds

5 hours for draining

5 days for curing

BEST USES
Table and cooking cheese

STORAGE
Keeps well for 2–3 months in the refrigerator when tightly wrapped

YIELD
About 1 pound fresh Feta

INGREDIENTS

1 gallon whole goat's milk

$\frac{1}{2}$ teaspoon powdered mesophilic starter

1 teaspoon liquid calf's rennet blended with $\frac{1}{4}$ cup cool water

4 tablespoons flake salt

HEATING AND RIPENING

Heat the milk in a double boiler for about 15 minutes, or until its temperature reaches 85°F. Blend in the mesophilic starter culture throughout the warm milk. Remove the pot from the burner, cover it, and allow the milk to ripen for 1 hour.

Blend the rennet in the cool water and add this liquid to the ripened mixture. Stir the milk with a whisk to make sure that the rennet is evenly distributed. Cover the pot again and allow the rennet to work for an hour, or until the curd shows a clean break when cut with a knife (no curd clings to the knife).

CUTTING AND DRAINING THE CURDS

Cut the curds into ¾-inch cubes and allow them to rest for 20 minutes, as the whey rises to the surface. Gently stir the curds for another 30 minutes, to keep them separated and work off additional whey.

Ladle the curds into a colander lined with a double thickness of cheesecloth large enough to tie the ends together. Tie the ends to form a draining bag. Then slip a dowel or chopsticks under the knot and hang the bag inside the cheese pot for draining, supported by the dowel.

Allow the curds to hang for about 5 hours, or until all of the whey has completely dripped off the bag. At this point, you should be able to feel a firm, solid mass of curds. If you can't, allow the curds to dry for another hour, then check for firmness again.

CURING THE CHEESE

Untie the bag and transfer the mass of Feta to a large bowl. Cut the cheese into slices about 1¼ inches thick, then into 1¼-inch cubes. Sprinkle the Feta cubes with the flake salt, making sure that all surfaces are covered. Loosely cover the bowl with a sheet of plastic wrap, top that with a towel, and allow the curds to steep in the flake salt for 4–5 days.

You now have a pound of fresh, zesty Feta for your table. Enjoy it in salad or serve it up with a platter of pita bread, mixed olives, and red grapes.

WHITE GOAT CHEDDAR

While Cheddar is a favorite in our house, the Cheddar made from goat's milk gets top billing. The cheddaring and stirring process, when married to goat's milk, offers a tangy cheese that transforms the food it encounters. This recipe creates a cheese that complements roasted vegetables, herbs, and spicy sauces.

LEVEL
Medium (requires a little handwork, but the process is less involved than with some Cheddars)

START TO FINISH
2½–3 hours for heating and ripening
12–15 hours or overnight for pressing
3 days for drying
30 days for aging

BEST USE
Good table and cooking cheese

STORAGE
4–6 weeks, tightly wrapped and refrigerated

YIELD
1 pound goat Cheddar

INGREDIENTS

1 gallon pasteurized whole goat's milk

2 tablespoons mesophilic starter culture

¾ teaspoon liquid rennet or ¼ rennet tablet in ¼ cup cool water

1 tablespoon coarse salt

TIP... *Although you can double this recipe, adjusting the ripening and cooking time, I recommend making a single recipe, from just one gallon of milk, until you have the knack for the whole process.*

HEATING AND RIPENING THE MILK

Heat the milk in a double boiler over medium-low heat for 20–30 minutes, or until the temperature reaches 90°F. Remove the pot from the heat and slowly stir in the mesophilic starter. Cover the pot and allow the milk to ripen for 30 minutes.

ADDING RENNET

If you are using dry rennet, crush it into powder with a spoon before adding it to the ¼ cup cool water. *If you are using liquid rennet,* simply blend it into the cool water with a whisk. Add the liquid to the ripened milk and slowly blend it throughout the mixture. Cover the pot and allow the rennet to set the milk for 30–45 minutes, or until the curd makes a clean break when cut with a knife.

CUTTING AND STIRRING THE CURDS

Using a curd knife, gently cut the curds into ½-inch cubes and allow them to settle for 30 minutes as the whey rises to the surface. (You may want to collect this goat whey for a small batch of ricotta or home-made bread.)

For another 30 minutes, increase the temperature from 90°F to 100°F, while *gently* turning the curds with your spoon—you are simply encouraging more whey to rise, allowing the cheese curds to firm up while remaining a loose mass.

For another 30 minutes, maintain the temperature and continue to turn the curds. Then, with a shallow ladle or spoon, slowly drain as much whey as possible and set the pot aside for 10 minutes so that the curds can settle a bit.

DRAINING THE CURDS

Place a colander lined with cheesecloth or buttercloth in a sterile basin, then ladle the curds into the colander. Allow them to drain for 15 minutes, or until the whey stops dripping.

Transfer the curds back to the cheese pot and break them up with your fingers, in order to prevent them from matting together. Sprinkle the salt over the curds, and blend it thoroughly into the mixture with a large slotted spoon.

PRESSING THE CURDS

Transfer the curds to a press lined with cheesecloth or buttercloth, then press the curds at 40 pounds of pressure for 12–15 hours or overnight. Take the cheese out of the press and unwrap it. The surface should be smooth and a little glossy, free of any cracks or splits (these would indicate that the cheese is too dry).

TIPS... *Cracks and splits may occur in this cheese if the milk is scant on fat, if the weather is too hot, or if the cheese has been overly stirred or pressed. Balance is one of the biggest factors in the development of this or any other good cheese.*

DRYING AND AGING THE CHEESE

Rub all surfaces of the Cheddar with a little salt and place the cheese on a flat rack. Allow it to air dry for 3 days, turning it once every 24 hours. At this point the Cheddar should show signs of forming its own rind. If this isn't apparent, allow it to sit for another 1–2 days.

Wrap the cheese in plastic wrap and allow it to age in the refrigerator for 30 days before cutting. You can let it sit for another 30–45 days, if you prefer a slightly stronger cheese.

TIP... *If a cheese develops an unwanted mold, advises the American Cheese Society, make a cut about $1/2$ inch below the mold and slice it away; the rest of the cheese will still be fine.*

CHEDDARING, *a process unique to making Cheddar, involves slicing the drained curds into strips and allowing them to set. Like the cheese, it takes its name from Cheddar, England, in Somerset, where the cheese originated.*

YELLOW AGED CHEDDAR

Cheddar's deep golden color and rich, sometimes nutty flavor make it one of England's finest cheeses. First produced in Somerset farmhouses, the cheese remained white until the later 1500s, when someone decided to add a pinch of saffron. (Some knowledgeable cheese aficionados will tell you that *real* Cheddar contains no added color.) Yellow Cheddar is a favorite partner of fruit, breads, and homemade enchiladas.

LEVEL
Medium (a process with a number of
steps, requiring some acquired skill,
patience, and pacing)

START TO FINISH
About 8 hours from start to cheese press

24 hours in the press

3 days for drying

45 days to 6 months for aging

BEST USE
Good table and cooking cheese

STORAGE
Keeps for up to 2 months after cutting,
in an airtight container in the refrigerator

YIELD
About 2 pounds Cheddar

INGREDIENTS

2 gallons whole pasteurized cow's milk

½ teaspoon mesophilic starter powder
or 4 tablespoons fresh starter

1 teaspoon liquid rennet in ¼ cup cool water

Liquid annato cheese coloring (optional)

Brick of cheese wax (unused wax can be stored)

TIP... *If you want to add a little color to your cheese,
try it with Cheddar, and try the whole process with
this recipe. Cheese is either white or strawlike in color,
depending on the diet of the animal producing the
milk. By and large, the hues commonly available from
commercial sources are artificial. Remember that a
little color—just two drops—will give a gallon of milk
plenty of additional glow. Less is definitely more here.*

HEATING AND RIPENING THE MILK

Warm the milk in a double boiler until the temperature reaches 85°F. Stir the mesophilic starter into the
liquid, remove the pot from the heat, cover, and allow
to ripen for 1 hour.

ADDING COLOR

If you wish to add a little color, do it now. The liquid
annato cheese coloring needs to be used *sparingly*,
however. Just 3–4 drops will be enough to add plenty
of golden color to the Cheddar here, with the standard being two drops of color per gallon of milk.

Add the color and gently stir it into the ripened milk
with a wire whisk. The milk won't show much of a
change, but the color is working. If you want a deeper
yellow, add 2 more drops. Allow the mixture to set for
5 minutes.

ADDING RENNET

Blend the liquid rennet into ¼ cup cool water and
add this to the ripening milk. Cover the pot and allow
it to sit for another 60 minutes, while the rennet
coagulates the mixture. Test the curd with a knife. It
should show a clean break.

WARMING, COOKING, AND DRAINING THE CURDS

Return the double boiler to the burner and increase
the heat just enough to warm the curds to 100°F, over
a period of 30–40 minutes—*only 2 degrees every 5–6
minutes*. Turn the curds occasionally with a slotted
spoon, in order to prevent them from matting.

Continue to stir the curds for another 30 minutes at
this temperature. Then remove the pot from the heat
and allow the curds to settle, as the whey rises to the
surface.

Place a colander lined with cheesecloth or buttercloth
in a sterile basin. Slowly pour in the hot curds and
allow them to drain for 15–20 minutes, or until the
whey stops dripping.

CHEDDARING THE CURDS

This step involves slicing and soaking the curds in warm water for about 2 hours, before cutting them into cubes. Turn the drained curds onto a clean cutting board, being careful to keep them intact as one mass. The mass should be firm and rather solid to the touch. (The results of adding a little too much color or increasing the heat too quickly will often not show up until you reach this stage. If you have a mass of curds that doesn't want to hold together, it's time to cut your losses and start over.)

Cut the curds into slices about 3 inches long and ½ inch thick. Transfer the curds back to the pot and allow it to sit in a sink of warm water (100°F) for 2 hours; during that time, turn the slices over every 30 minutes.

This part of the process firms the curds and makes them a bit rubbery to the touch after 2 hours. A piece should spring back slightly when you press it between your thumb and forefinger.

MILLING AND SALTING THE CURDS

Remove the pot from the warm water and use the curd knife to cut the slices into ¾-inch cubes. Return the pot to the warm water and stir or turn the curds with a slotted spoon for about 30–45 minutes. This will expel a little additional whey and keep the curds from matting as they continue to harden.

Take the pot out of the warm water and sprinkle the curds with 2 tablespoons of salt. Blend the salt throughout the mixture with a slotted spoon.

TIP... *Slowly milling, or stirring, cooked curds helps expel and evaporate whey. Stirring vigorously creates too much heat and activity—and out goes the fat that gives cheese its proper flavor and texture.*

Milling and salting the cheese

PRESSING THE CURDS

The curds will need to be pressed for about 36 hours—1½ days. Ladle the curds into a cheese-press mold lined with cheesecloth or buttercloth. Fold the cloth over the curds, then apply 40 pounds of pressure for 12 hours. Flip the cheese and press at 40 pounds for another 12 hours, and then again 12 hours later, so that the cheese gets pressed and turned 3 times in 36 hours.

Take the cheese out of the press and remove the cloth. It should peel away very readily, and your cheese should be smooth and devoid of cracks or splits on all surfaces. Transfer the cheese to a mat or flat rack and allow it to air dry for 3 days, turning it once a day.

After 3 days, the cheese should show signs of a natural rind. Melt a little cheese wax in a small pan, then brush the wax on all surfaces of the cheese until it is completely sealed. (Any unwaxed area is an open invitation for unwanted bacteria and the wrong variety of moldy cheese.)

AGING THE CHEESE

Allow the cheese to age in a cool room or the refrigerator (at 55°F) for 45 days before cutting. You can create a richer, sharper Cheddar if you allow it to age for 6–12 months (if you can keep your hands off it).

SAGE CHEDDAR

Cheddar cheese takes on a whole new dimension when you combine it with herbs. Once you've tried making standard yellow Cheddar, you may want to experiment with chives, thyme, or sage. The flavor and scent of homemade Cheddar made with fresh garden sage rivals its commercially produced cousins.

LEVEL
Medium

START TO FINISH
See recipe for white goat Cheddar or yellow Cheddar and add about 10 minutes

BEST USE
Good table cheese

STORAGE
1 or 2 months, depending on base cheese

YIELD
1 or 2 pounds sage cheddar, depending on base cheese

NOTE: *The assumption of this recipe is that you are making a sage variation of either the white goat Cheddar or the yellow Cheddar in the preceding recipes. Adding sage becomes a step in the process, at a different stage for each Cheddar. For both cheeses, it is the last step before transferring the curds to the cheese press.*

PREPARING THE SAGE

Simmer ¼ cup of freshly chopped sage in ½ cup of water in a small saucepan for 3–5 minutes, or until the water begins to turn green. Remove the saucepan from the heat and set it aside to cool for 20 minutes.

WHEN TO ADD THE SAGE

If you are making the white Cheddar, add the sage and its broth when salting the curds after stirring. *If you are making the yellow Cheddar,* add the sage and its broth once you have milled the curds and turned in the salt.

Adding sage to curds of fresh yellow cheddar

HOLLAND GOUDA

Gouda, pronounced "how'-da" in its native Holland, has remarkable properties for long-term storage. This straightforward, creamy cheese needs little embellishment, although many cheese lovers enjoy smoked Gouda and Gouda made with caraway. It also marries well with peppercorns and a variety of herbs such as sage, apple mint, and parsley. For one of the best apple cobblers you'll ever taste or serve, donate some of your homemade Gouda to a Gouda Apple Cobbler (page 134).

LEVEL
Medium (a number of steps, and a full day's work)

START TO FINISH
2 hours for ripening
1¼ hours for cooking and draining
3½ hours for pressing
2 weeks for drying
3–6 months for aging

BEST USE
Good table and cooking cheese. Aged Gouda makes a great grating cheese.

STORAGE
Keeps for 2–6 months when sealed and refrigerated. As it continues to dry out, Gouda becomes less a slicing, and more a grating, cheese.

YIELD
1½–2 pounds Gouda

INGREDIENTS

2 gallons whole cow's or goat's milk

½ cup homemade mesophilic starter or 1 packet mesophilic starter powder

1 teaspoon liquid rennet in ¼ cup cool water

Brine solution: 4 cups salt in 1 gallon water

Cheese wax

TIP... *Although Gouda can be successfully rendered from goat's milk, I've found that whole cow's milk works best. It contains more fat than goat's milk, and my family prefers the flavor for eating as well as cooking.*

HEATING AND RIPENING THE MILK

Warm 2 gallons of whole milk in a double boiler over medium heat for 20–30 minutes, until the temperature reaches 90°F. Add the mesophilic starter culture and thoroughly blend it into the warm milk with a whisk or slotted spoon.

Blend the liquid rennet with the cool water. With a wire whisk, lightly but thoroughly mix the rennet into the milk and top stir the surface. Remove the pot from the heat, cover, and allow the milk to ripen for 2 hours. Test the curds with a knife—if they show a clean break, they are ready for cooking and draining. If curd clings to the knife, the mixture may need to ripen for another 30 minutes or longer.

COOKING THE CURDS

Return the double boiler to the burner and increase the temperature of the curds over the next 30 minutes from 90°F to 100°F. *The heat should increase by about 2 degrees every 4–5 minutes.* (Heating too quickly will jeopardize the flavor and texture of your cheese.)

WASHING THE CURDS

Heat the curds, stirring them continuously, maintaining a temperature of 100°F. You are now ready to drain the curds of whey and replace the whey with water of the same temperature. (Water that is hotter or colder than the existing 100°F can cause a breakdown in the process of coagulation.)

Drain the curds with a measuring cup until most of the whey has been removed from the surface. Measure the whey as you collect it, because you will replace it with an equal amount of water. The amount of whey can vary somewhat from one batch of milk to the next, but you can expect to remove about 6–8 cups of whey. Replace it with an equal amount of 100° water.

Stir the fresh warm water into the curds, then give them a few minutes to absorb it. Continue to turn the curds, so that more whey rises to the surface, along with any material that can interfere with the smoothness Gouda lovers cherish. (You are literally rinsing, or washing, the curds.)

Repeat this process of washing the curds a total of 3 times, or every 15 minutes for 45 minutes. Then pour off any additional whey and set the pot aside. Let the curds settle for about 10 minutes until they form one mass.

PRESSING THE CHEESE

Line a 2-pound cheese-press mold with cheesecloth or buttercloth, and try to pour the curds into the mold in one mass. (Breaking the curds up can interfere with the Gouda holding together during the pressing.) Add any followers that the press requires and apply 15 pounds of pressure for 30 minutes.

Flip the Gouda and apply 15 pounds of pressure for another 30 minutes. Turn the cheese a third time, and apply 30 pounds of pressure for $3\frac{1}{2}$ hours.

BRINING AND DRYING THE CHEESE

Release the pressure gauge, take the cheese out of the mold, and unwrap it. The surface of the Gouda should be smooth and free of any cracks or splits. Such cracks or splits may result from unreliable milk, rushing the stirring, or overpressing. (Do not despair if you find them. Your outer rind may end up a little too dry, but the waxing should keep things stable while the cheese continues to age.)

Combine the salt and water in a basin or bowl and place the Gouda in this brine. The cheese will float, and it should stay in this bath for about 3 hours. Turn or flip the cheese once an hour for this period.

Remove the cheese from the brine and pat it dry with a lint-free towel. Place the cheese on a mat or flat rack and store it at 50˚F in the refrigerator or a cool room for approximately 3 weeks to air dry. Turn the cheese daily as it continues to dry and form a soft, natural rind.

WAXING AND AGING THE CHEESE

Covered with a thin coat of wax, Gouda continues to age without drying out too much. Melt a little cheese wax and brush it on all surfaces of the cheese. The wax dries almost as soon as it's applied, and your Gouda will be ready for further aging in minutes.

Age this cheese for 3–6 months, at 50˚F and 85–90 percent humidity before cutting, and you will be rewarded with a creamy, flavorful cheese. If you prefer a deeper, more resonant flavor, you can age your Gouda for 9 months or even longer.

Cheese wax is easy to apply and dries quickly. You can brush on two or three coats of wax in fifteen minutes, while turning and handling the cheese, without concern for burnt fingers.

ROMANO

Revered as the first pasta cheese still in existence, Romano was known as *caciocavallo* (horseback cheese) as early as the first century A.D. Pecorino Romano—sheep's milk cheese—is produced in Lazio, outside of Rome, and famously in Tuscany. When sheep's milk isn't available, the cow's milk variety of this recipe produces an equally sharp, zesty cheese that will last in your refrigerator for months.

INGREDIENTS

- ¼ teaspoon capilase powder dissolved in ¼ cup cool water
- 2 gallons 2 percent cow's milk
- ¼ cup fresh, or 1 teaspoon powdered, thermophilic starter
- ¾ teaspoon liquid rennet mixed with ¼ cup cool water
- Salt brine: 4 cups (2 pounds) salt blended with 1 gallon water

MAKING THE CAPILASE SOLUTION

Blend the capilase enzyme powder with the water and set aside.

HEATING AND RIPENING THE MILK

Warm the milk in a double boiler over medium-low heat until the thermometer reads 88°F. Remove the pot from the heat and thoroughly (*and slowly*) stir in the thermophilic starter culture. Cover the pot and allow the milk to ripen for 30 minutes.

Stir in the capilase liquid, making sure that it blends evenly in the ripened milk. Gently stir in the rennet liquid and cover the pot again. Allow the rennet to work for 30 minutes, or until the curd shows a clean break when tested with a knife.

LEVEL
Medium (without some of the time-consuming steps of some hard cheeses)

START TO FINISH
20 minutes for heating and ripening
30 minutes for coagulation
20 minutes for setting the curds
45–60 minutes for cooking and draining
12–15 hours for pressing
12 hours for brining
6–12 months for aging

BEST USES
Cooking and grating

STORAGE
Keeps well for several months wrapped and refrigerated

YIELD
2 pounds Romano

CUTTING, COOKING, AND DRAINING THE CURDS

Cut the curds into ½-inch cubes and allow them to rest for 20 minutes.

Return the pot of curds to the range and, for another 30 minutes, increase the heat under the pot, *gently* stirring and turning the curds, until the thermometer reads 115°F. Turn the curds gently for another 10 minutes, then transfer to a colander lined with cheesecloth or buttercloth. Let everything settle for 10 minutes, while you prepare the cheese press.

PRESSING AND BRINING THE CHEESE

Line a 2-pound cheese-press mold with cheesecloth or buttercloth, and pour in the curds. Cover with the remaining cloth. Top with followers and apply 5 pounds of pressure for 15 minutes to one side. Then turn the cheese and apply 5 pounds of pressure for 15 minutes to the other side.

Mixing brine for floating the Romano

TIP... *Romano wouldn't be Romano without the sharp flavor that gives pasta, pizza, and so many other dishes their distinctive bite. The secret lies in an enzyme called capilase. It reacts to heat and culture to break down complex carbohydrates in the lactose, or sugar, in milk.*

Take the Romano out of the mold and gently peel away the soaked cloth. Rewrap the cheese with a fresh cloth, then return it to the press. Apply 15 pounds of pressure for 2 hours. Turn the cheese and press it at 30 pounds of pressure for 15 hours.

To make a brine solution, mix the salt with the water in a stainless-steel basin and stir. Then allow the water to settle. A layer of salt at the bottom of the basin tells you the water is properly salt saturated.

Float the Romano in the brine for 12 hours.

DRYING AND CURING

Remove the Romano from the brine, pat it dry with a clean cheesecloth or buttercloth, and place it on a cheese mat or flat rack for drying.

Transfer the fresh cheese to a cool room or your refrigerator and allow it to cure at 55–60°F and 90 percent humidity, as measured by your hygrometer, for 6–10 months. Turn the cheese daily and check it for surface mold. If you detect a bit of growth, simply wipe it away with cheesecloth or buttercloth dipped in cider vinegar. You can also rub a little olive oil onto the surface of the Romano—the surface should be lightly coated without feeling greasy; a little oil goes a long way. This enlivens the flavor of the natural rind and helps keep the cheese moist.

LEVEL
Medium (about 3 days of preparation)

START TO FINISH
30–45 minutes for heating and ripening

30–45 for rennet/coagulation

45–60 minutes for cooking and draining curds

15–18 hours (overnight) for molding and pressing

10–12 hours (overnight) for brining

6–12 months for aging

BEST USES
A good table cheese when young and an excellent cooking and grating cheese when more aged

STORAGE
Keeps well for up to 3 months when tightly wrapped and refrigerated; dries out quickly when exposed to air (becomes flat and difficult to grate for cooking)

YIELD
2 pounds Parmesan

PARMESAN

Since its development in the Emilia Romagna region of Italy 700 years ago, Parmesan has topped pizza, rigatoni, soup, bread, and salad. For a unique and delicious bread to serve with your homemade Parmesan, make Lemon Mozzarella with Parmesan Crostini (page 119). Or for a special dinner, try the impressive and elegant Three-Cheese Herb Torte (page 116).

TIP... *The Stresa Convention of 1952 laid down guidelines and protection for cheese-making countries. The names Parmesan and Gorgonzola, for example, could be used only on cheese produced in Italy, Roquefort only on cheese produced in France. The convention was signed by most major European cheese-producing countries.*

INGREDIENTS

$1/4$ teaspoon kid lipase powder mixed in $1/4$ cup water

1   gallon whole goat's milk

1   gallon skim cow's milk

4   ounces fresh , or 1 teaspoon powdered, thermophilic starter

1   teaspoon liquid calf's rennet blended with $1/4$ cup cool water

Brine: 4 cups salt in 1 gallon water

TIP... *Lipase is an enzyme that helps break down sugar, which adds flavor to cheese. Even though Parmesan can be delicious when made without a little lipase, the tangy piquant flavors lent by this enzyme cast a strong argument for its use.*

MAKING THE LIPASE SOLUTION

Make the lipase solution as your first step, because it needs to sit and ripen for about 30–45 minutes before you add it to the curds. Blend the lipase and the water and set aside.

HEATING THE MILK

Mix the cow's and goat's milk in a double boiler and warm to 90°F. Turn off the heat, cover the pot, and allow the milk to ripen for 30–45 minutes. Add the lipase solution and blend it into the milk with a whisk or slotted spoon. Stir slowly for a minute or two, so that the lipase gets blended into all of the liquid.

RENNETING AND COAGULATION

Maintain the temperature and stir in the rennet solution. Cover the pot again and allow the rennet to work for 30–45 minutes, or until the curds show a clean break when cut with a knife. Once the curds are firm, cut them into $1/2$-inch to $5/8$-inch cubes.

COOKING AND DRAINING THE CURDS

Set the pot aside and allow the curds to settle, as the whey rises to the surface. Then slowly increase the heat under the pot until the curds reach 100°F. Stir the curds slowly but constantly and continue to heat the mixture, until the thermometer reads 120°F.

Continue stirring for another 20–25 minutes, or until the curds shrink to the size of grains of rice. Pick up a piece of curd and squeeze it between your thumb and index finger. It should be a bit springy and may even squeak a little under pressure, signs that the curds are dry and firm enough to drain and press. If they don't feel firm with this test, continue to stir and cook for another 15 minutes before testing again.

Transfer the curds to a colander lined with cheese-cloth or buttercloth and allow them to drain for 20 minutes.

MOLDING AND PRESSING THE CHEESE

Pour the curds into a 2-pound cheese-press mold that you've lined with cheesecloth or buttercloth. Cover the curds with the excess cloth and top with any followers you might need.

Apply 5 pounds of pressure for 10 minutes, then flip the cheese and apply 5 pounds of pressure to the other side for 10 minutes.

Turn the cheese a third time and apply 15 pounds of pressure for 1 hour; then turn it again and apply 15 pounds of pressure to the other side for 1 hour. (Turning the cheese so many times ensures that the moisture inside the cheese is evenly distributed.)

Remove the cheese from the mold and unwrap it. Line the mold with a fresh cloth, place the cheese back in the press, and cover it with the excess cloth. Apply 20 pounds of pressure for 12–15 hours.

Take the Parmesan out of the press and remove the cloth. It should peel away fairly easily, and the surface of your cheese should be free of cracks and splits, signs that your cheese could be a bit too dry. (Even if you have cracks or splits, the cheese is edible, and you'll improve your technique on your next batch.) Set the cheese aside while you make the brine.

BRINING AND AGING THE CHEESE

Combine the salt and the slightly warm water in a stainless-steel basin and stir. Then let the brine rest for 3–4 minutes. A layer of salt on the bottom of the basin signifies that the water is totally saturated. Allow the cheese to float uncovered in the brine for 12 hours at room temperature. Then turn it over and allow it to float for another 12 hours.

Remove the Parmesan from the brine and place it on a rack or cheese mat. Parmesan ages readily at 55°F and a controlled humidity of 85 percent, in your refrigerator or a cool room—use a hygrometer to check and maintain a stable temperature and level of humidity. As it ages, the Parmesan will form a natural rind and may grow a little mold on the surface. Wipe away the mold with a clean cheesecloth or buttercloth, and turn your cheese once a week.

You can cut into your homemade cheese after 3 months, but greater flavor awaits if you can hold out for 6–9 months of curing.

Parmesan floats in brine for 24 hours before curing.

RACLETTE

Unless you live in Switzerland, where the cows graze on sweet mountain grasses, you cannot produce the flavor of a "true" raclette—just a great-quality cheese that melts in a very satisfying fashion for a hearty winter lunch. This raclette has a nutty, yet slightly sweet and pungent flavor. Its texture lends itself to cheese pancakes, as shown in the photo, and to casseroles and potatoes. As a table cheese, marry it with fruit and bread.

LEVEL
Fairly difficult (requires considerable time)

START TO FINISH
1½ hours for heating and ripening

45–60 minutes for renneting and coagulation

1 hour for cooking the curds

1 hour for draining and setting

3 days for curing

2–4 months for aging

BEST USES
Good table and excellent melting cheese

STORAGE
Stores well for months when tightly wrapped and refrigerated, but dries out fairly quickly if not properly sealed

YIELD
2 pounds raclette

INGREDIENTS

2 gallons whole cow's milk

¼ cup fresh, or 1 teaspoon powdered, mesophilic starter

¾ teaspoon liquid rennet mixed with ¼ cup cool water

Salt brine: 4 cups salt in 1 gallon water

Bacterial linens

TIP... *This raclette works best with raw milk that you pasteurize yourself; you will produce a still delicious yet slightly softer cheese from homogenized whole milk.*

HEATING AND RIPENING

Note: It's important to refrain from heating either milk or curds too quickly here. The cheese simply won't hold together if you rush.

Warm the milk for about 30 minutes in a double boiler until the temperature reaches 88°F. Slowly stir in the mesophilic starter culture, blending it well throughout the milk. Cover and set aside to ripen for 1 hour.

Blend the rennet into the ripening milk. Allow the rennet to work undisturbed for 1 hour, or until the curds show a clean break when tested with a knife.

Cut the curds into ¼-inch cubes and allow them to settle to the bottom of the pot, as the whey rises to the surface.

FOREWORKING AND COOKING THE CURDS

Before you begin foreworking—stirring the lukewarm curds before cooking—heat about 2 quarts of water to a temperature of 140°F. Maintain the water at this temperature for washing the curds later.

Slowly stir the curds with a large ladle or spoon. (This will dispel more of the moisture and prevent the curds from sticking together.)

Skim whey from the surface of the curds with a measuring cup, keeping track of the amount as you go. Replace the drained whey with an equal amount of the water you've preheated to 140ºF, and gently stir the curds as you add the water, until the curds reach a temperature of 100°F. Be sure the temperature doesn't rise above 100°F, or your cheese won't solidify properly.

Continue to stir the curds for another 30–45 minutes at 100°F until they firm up. Then set the pot aside and allow the curds to rest for another 30 minutes.

DRAINING AND BRINING THE CHEESE

Tilt the pot and carefully ladle or spoon the excess whey from the curds. Then set the curds aside to acidify for 1 more hour.

In the meantime, prepare brine by blending 4 cups of salt into 1 gallon of slightly warm water in a large pot or stainless-steel basin. Gently stir the solution for about 5 minutes before you allow the contents to settle. You should be able to see a layer of salt at the bottom, which means that the water is completely salt saturated and ready for the freshly processed raclette.

Place the raclette in the brine and allow it to float for 12 hours, turning once after 6 hours of soaking. Remove the cheese from the brine and pat dry with a clean cheesecloth or buttercloth.

Transfer the raclette to a rack or cheese mat and allow it to air dry for an hour.

CURING THE CHEESE

Add 1 teaspoon of bacterial linens to 1 quart of water, in an atomizer. Shake well. Spray all surfaces of the raclette and place it on the cheese mat or rack in the refrigerator or a cool room (55°F and 85 percent humidity). Allow it to rest for 2 days, turning once each day. On day 3, spray the cheese again.

You should now be able to detect a slight reddish-brown mold. Allow the raclette to age for another 2 months, as it steeps with flavor and forms a natural rind. If you prefer a cheese with a stronger flavor, give it an additional 2 months.

This cheese is especially good for warming bodies as well as souls on a cold-weather day.

For a cheese pancake, cut raclette into thin slices and melt in a nonstick pan.

THANKS...

I developed this recipe from the Wisby Corporation's guidelines for raclette, which cheese expert Jim Mildbrand so generously shared with me.

BABY SWISS

It's safe to say that most people do not know either how the holes get in Swiss cheese, or that Swiss cheese comes in many varieties—grand Swiss, Emmenthaler, Alpine Lace, Baby Swiss, and more. The "eyes," or holes, in baby Swiss are miniatures of the eyes of other Swiss varieties—thus the name. You'll find two tasty dishes in this book to show off your homemade Serenely Swiss Fondue (page 109) and Swiss Onion Flatbread (page 117).

LEVEL
Difficult (about 3–3½ days to get the cheese ready for curing)

START TO FINISH
1 hour for heating and ripening

30 minutes for renneting

3 hours for cutting and foreworking

15–18 hours (overnight) for pressing

8–12 hours for brining

5 days for curing

2–3 weeks for drying

3–6 months for aging

BEST USES
Eating and cooking

STORAGE
Keeps well for up to 3 months (sometimes longer, depending on the climate) when wrapped tightly and refrigerated

YIELD
2 pounds Swiss

INGREDIENTS

2 gallons whole cow's milk

½ teaspoon thermophilic powder, or 1 ounce homemade starter

¾–1 teaspoon proprionic powder

½ teaspoon liquid rennet in ¼ cup water

Salt brine: 4 cups (2 pounds) salt in 1 gallon water

TIP... Proprionic powder, *like other chemically reactive agents, needs cold storage until you're ready to use it. Buy a freeze-dried variety sealed in a foil packet; it will keep in the freezer for 3 to 4 months.*

HEATING, RIPENING, AND RENNETING

Warm 2 gallons of whole milk in a double boiler for 20–30 minutes, until the milk reaches 90-92°F. Stir in the thermophilic culture with a wire whisk or slotted spoon.

Use a measuring cup to remove about ¼–⅓ of the warm milk from the pot. Blend the proprionic powder into this milk, return it to the pot, and gently blend it throughout the entire mixture.

Remove the double boiler from the heat, cover it, and allow the milk to ripen for 20–30 minutes. Add the rennet water and blend it into the ripening milk. Cover the pot again and allow the curds to form and coagulate for 30 minutes. The curds should show a clean break when you test them with a knife.

FOREWORKING AND COOKING THE CURDS

Maintain the ripening temperature of 90–92°F and slowly turn and stir the curds for 45–60 minutes, or until little or no whey is evident near the surface and sides of the pot. (*Foreworking* is simply the stirring of lukewarm curds before cooking.)

For the next 45–50 minutes, heat the curds gradually (*1°F every 1–2 minutes*) until the temperature reaches 115°F. Continue to stir the curds for 20–30 minutes longer, to firm them up for the press. The curds are ready if they break apart easily when you rub a tablespoon or two between your finger and the palm of your hand. If they don't break apart readily, allow them to cook for another 10–20 minutes, until they firm up and want to separate.

TIP... *The first time I made this cheese, I was amazed to see little holes developing on its surface (even though I knew I was making Swiss cheese). The bacteria that goes into the ripening milk makes gas, and the gas makes the holes, or eyes, in Swiss cheese. Now you know.*

MOLDING AND PRESSING THE CHEESE

Be sure to keeps things moving, because the curds need to mold and press while hot. Ladle or pour the curds into a cheese-press mold lined with cheese-cloth or buttercloth. Cover the curds with the cloth, and add followers if you need them.

Apply 10 pounds of pressure for 30 minutes, then flip the cheese and apply 10 pounds of pressure for 30 minutes again. At this point, your cloth will be soaked with whey and small particles of curd. You should be able to gently peel away the wet cloth; then wrap the molded curds in a fresh one.

Return the wrapped cheese to the mold and apply 15 pounds of pressure for 12–14 hours, or overnight. Remove the pressed Swiss from its mold and its bandage and set it aside to rest while you prepare the brine.

Swiss cheese fresh from the press. An occasional swipe with a dry salted cheesecloth encourages the surface to continue to dry and harden, as it begins to form its own natural rind.

BRINING, CURING, AND AGING THE CHEESE

To make brine, combine 4 cups (2 pounds) of coarse salt with a gallon of barely warm water. Place the ingredients in a large stainless steel pot and stir everything together for roughly 5 minutes with a whisk or slotted spoon, dissolving as much of the salt as possible. Allow the water to settle. You should see a layer of salt at the bottom of the basin, which means that the water has been completely saturated.

Place the cheese in the brine and allow it to steep in the refrigerator for 8–12 hours, or overnight. Prepare a lint-free, salt-soaked cloth by immersing the cloth in salt water (¼ cup salt in 1 quart water), wringing it out, and hanging it to dry.

Take the cheese out of the brine, wipe it dry with the dry, salt-soaked cloth, and allow it to set in the refrigerator or a cool room for 5 days. (A dry salted cloth helps to prevent mold formation on the surface and to promote the formation of a natural rind.) Turn the cheese 2 times a day, or every 10–12 hours.

Your Swiss is now ready to air dry for 14–21 days in a warm (70–72°F), draft-free spot in your kitchen or pantry, *whichever maintains enough heat and the humidity required for the formation of holes, or eyes, in the cheese.*

It's important to check and turn the cheese daily, to ensure the even distribution of internal moisture. Continue to wipe the outside surface with a lint-free, salt-soaked dry cloth.

At 18–21 days, the Swiss should be noticeably swollen (from all the gas inside), with eye formation showing on the surface. Transfer the cheese to the refrigerator or a cool room where the climate can be controlled to 50°F and 85 percent humidity; age it for 3–6 months or longer. Check the humidity daily and, if it drops, place a bowl of warm water next to the cheese. The rind will naturally show some discoloration throughout this process, but if you see any surface mold, simply wipe it away with a dry salted cloth. Turn your cheese every other day.

LEVEL
Difficult (long cooking time)

START TO FINISH
10–14 hours. Don't plan on doing anything else with your day, and plan to get an early start, because there really isn't any way to break up the process—a good cheese to make with a friend.

BEST USE
Good table and melting cheese

STORAGE
Keeps well in the refrigerator more than 6 months when properly sealed

YIELD
1–1¼ pounds gjetost

GJETOST

You make this versatile Norwegian cheese (pronounced "yay toast") from whey, so plan ahead. (This is where saving the whey from white goat Cheddar comes in handy.) The recipe relies entirely on nature, the quality of the milk, and heat. In texture and color—thick or thin, dark or light—you can alter Gjetost to suit your personal taste. Eat it by itself or with fruit and bread or heated to complement soups and stews. To achieve even greater renown as a cheese maker, make the recipe for Gjetost Pizza (page 122).

INGREDIENTS AND EQUIPMENT

2 gallons whey from pasteurized whole goat's milk

Molds, 4–6 ounces each

HEATING AND COOKING THE WHEY

It's a good idea to have two pots for making gjetost— one to cook and boil the whey, and a second ready for the whey once it's been processed in the blender.

No double boiler is required for this recipe. Warm the pot of whey directly over medium heat until it comes to a full, but not rolling, boil.

Maintain the temperature and continue to cook the whey, skimming away foam from the surface with a slotted spoon. Set the foam aside and allow it to cool for 15 minutes before refrigerating it. (You will return the cooled foam to the pot once the whey has reduced in volume.).

Reduce the heat to medium low and continue to cook and stir the whey for the next 8–10 hours, slowly reducing the liquid by about 2 quarts, leaving about 1½ gallons of whey in the pot.

Continue to stir the whey to prevent it from sticking, and add the reserved and chilled foam. Cook for another 15–20 minutes, or until the whey thickens and begins to look like a light butterscotch pudding. Remove the pot from the stove and allow the liquid to set for 2–3 minutes.

PROCESSING THE WHEY

Carefully pour the hot whey into a food processor or blender, a batch at a time. Pulse each batch of whey for about 30–45 seconds, then transfer it to the second pot, until all the whey has been processed.

SIMMERING THE PROCESSED WHEY

The hardest part is over—you now need only about another hour to finish thickening the gjetost and pouring it into molds.

Fill a basin or the kitchen sink with water and ice cubes. (Once the whey gets thick, you'll transfer the pot to the ice water for quick cool-down.) To ready your molds for the processed whey, place them in a shallow, heat-proof pan and place the pan on a mat or kitchen towel that can absorb heat (the cooked gjetost will be extremely hot as you pour it into its containers).

Bring the whey to a boil for a second time, over medium heat. Stir it slowly and constantly to prevent it from sticking. Keep stirring as the consistency gets thicker (otherwise, the gjetost can develop granules that stick to the pot). Your goal: cheese the consistency of cooking caramel or fudge.

COOLING THE CHEESE

Transfer the pot to the ice water and stir the thickened cheese for 2–3 minutes, or until cool enough to pour into the molds without bubbling over.

Allow the cheese to set for 8–10 hours before removing from the molds. Serve immediately or wrap in plastic and refrigerate.

During the early stages of cheese making, Gjetost has the color and consistency of thick butterscotch pudding; once cured, it retains a light, creamy caramel flavor.

recipes for extravagant cheese fare

appetizers

SERENELY SWISS FONDUE

Cheese is the very heart of the Swiss diet, and fondue provides the centerpiece for many meals. This simple, creamy, yet tangy mixture bubbling over a flame takes the chill out of winter and the edge off hunger. Classic fondue combines 1½ cups Gruyère, 1½ cups Emmenthaler, and ½ cup Appenzeller, but the recipe here allows you to substitute your own fine homemade cheeses for a fondue worthy of more than a yodel or two.

SERVING TIP: *I fold the prosciutto or ham into small tubes and pierce them with a toothpick for easy dipping.*

SPECIAL EQUIPMENT (OPTIONAL)

Fondue pot, fondue forks

INGREDIENTS

3½ cups Swiss, grated

1 cup Muenster or brick, grated

2–3 tablespoons all-purpose flour

1 clove garlic, minced

1 cup dry white wine (I prefer a Neuchâtel or Chablis)

2 tablespoons Dijon mustard

1 teaspoon fresh lemon juice

½ teaspoon finely ground white pepper

½ teaspoon dried onion

Dash cayenne (optional)

TIP: *Small crockpots work very well for cheese fondues, especially when serving a party buffet, because they maintain an even temperature over an indefinite period of time.*

INGREDIENTS FOR DIPPING

2 cups bread cubes, 2 sliced fresh pears, 2 sliced apples, 2 ounces prosciutto or other ham, sliced to taste

METHOD

In a large glass bowl, toss the grated cheese with the flour until coated. Set aside.

In a 2-quart fondue pot or other enamel-coated pot, heat the garlic and wine over a medium flame for 5 minutes. Add the cheese, 1 cup at a time, and heat until soft and easy to stir. Add the mustard, lemon juice, pepper, onion, and cayenne, stirring constantly for another 3 minutes. Keep the pot over a low flame and serve with bread, fruit, and prosciutto.

PREP TIME: 15–20 minutes
YIELD: 5 cups fondue
SERVES: 4–6

DANISH SESAME TWISTS

Although Danish blue plays well as solo entertainment, marrying it into baked cheese twists won't have you singing the blues. Store the twists in an airtight container for crispness and flavor for up to 2 weeks. This recipe is easily doubled and made in advance for a larger group of guests at your table.

INGREDIENTS

¾ cup Danish blue cheese, firmly packed

½ cup bread flour

2 tablespoons cornstarch

3 tablespoons unsalted butter or margarine, softened

⅛ teaspoon fine salt

¼ teaspoon ground green pepper

½ teaspoon lemon zest

1 tablespoon sesame seeds

METHOD

In a blender or food processor, combine the blue cheese, flour, cornstarch, butter, salt, green pepper, and lemon zest. Pulse for 2–3 minutes, or until all the ingredients are well blended.

Turn the dough out into a medium bowl and cover tightly with plastic wrap. Refrigerate for at least 8 hours, or overnight.

To assemble the twists, first preheat the oven to 375°F. Line a baking sheet with parchment paper or other bread-liner paper. Turn the dough out onto a floured surface. Roll the dough into a rectangle about 8 x 8 inches. Cut the rectangle horizontally, forming two halves of 4 x 8 inches. With a pastry cutter or sharp knife, cut the dough into strips about ½ inch wide. Twist each piece once or twice to create a spiral of dough.

Transfer the strips to the baking sheet and sprinkle with the sesame seeds.

Bake the twists for 10–15 minutes, or until crisp and golden. Transfer them to a wire rack to cool until slightly warm. Serve immediately, or allow to rest until completely cool for storage.

PREP TIME: 30 minutes
YIELD: Up to 36 cheese twists

CAMEMBERT PHYLLO

Don't be too quick to dismiss the rind of this creamy, full-flavored cheese—conduct a taste test first. Although the rind can sometimes be bitter, it can also be quite mild, and it lends an interesting bit of texture to the molded cheese within. Try this cheese with mixed raspberries and almonds, at rest in a blanket of warm, golden phyllo. Add it to a platter of sliced pears, yellow-delicious apples, and crusty bread for a simple, elegant lunch.

INGREDIENTS

1½ cups homemade mixed berry conserve

¼ cup chopped almonds

Whole 8-ounce Camembert

4 ounces melted, unsalted butter

3 large (12x15-inch) sheets phyllo dough, refrigerated

MIXED BERRY CONSERVE

1 cup whole red raspberries, rinsed and drained

1 cup whole blackberries, rinsed and drained

1 cup sugar

Juice of half a lemon

METHOD

Press the berries through a sieve or food mill to remove the seeds. Pour the berry pulp, sugar, and lemon juice into a 1-quart saucepan and cook over medium heat. Bring the berry mixture to a low boil and continue to cook for 20 minutes, stirring frequently to avoid sticking. Remove the pan from the heat and set aside to cool.

Remove the Camembert from the refrigerator and set aside while assembling the phyllo. Heat the oven to 375°F.

In a small saucepan, melt the butter and set aside. Remove the phyllo from the refrigerator. Brush a little of the melted butter onto the bottom of a glass baking dish and follow with a sheet of phyllo. Brush the phyllo with butter and add the two remaining sheets.

Spoon ¼ cup of the berry conserve onto the phyllo, where you plan to place the Camembert, giving the cheese a berry base. With a sharp knife, cut away a little of the top rind. Place the Camembert atop the conserve. Spoon the remaining berry mixture on top of the cheese and add the chopped almonds.

Fold the sides of the phyllo so that they cover the entire cheese round; bring the phyllo ends to the top. Brush all sides of the phyllo with the remaining butter. Bake for 15–20 minutes, or until the phyllo is slightly golden and the cheese remains soft, yet slightly firm.

Remove the cheese from the oven and allow it to rest for 3–5 minutes before serving. Serve warm.

PREP TIME: 1 hour
YIELD: 8–10 ounces
SERVES: 4–6

STILTON SPRING SALAD

The elegant Stilton marries the flavor of blue cheese with the taste and consistency of a soft Cheddar, an ideal match for this recipe's spring greens and young garlic. You can easily double it for a larger group of guests.

PREP NOTE: *You can make the lemon cream dressing 3–4 days ahead. If you do, be sure to take it out of the refrigerator to warm up a little while you assemble the salad.*

SALAD INGREDIENTS

    4 cups mixed baby greens

    2 cups young leaf lettuce

    3 scallions or stems of green garlic, chopped

    1 cup celery, chopped

    ¼ cup canned mandarin orange sections, drained

    ¼ cup red seedless grapes, rinsed and halved

    4 ounces Stilton, cubed

      Fresh lemon cream dressing

TIP: *Mixed baby greens can be found in most supermarkets, either packaged or loose, and sometimes called "mesclun" or "mesclun blend."*

LEMON CREAM DRESSING INGREDIENTS

    ¼ cup safflower oil

    ¾ cup sour cream

    1 tablespoon freshly grated lemon zest

    1 tablespoon fresh lemon juice

    ½ teaspoon salt

    ¼ teaspoon white pepper

    1 clove garlic, minced

    1 tablespoon fresh parsley, minced

    1 tablespoon crumbled Stilton

METHOD FOR THE DRESSING

Place the oil, sour cream, lemon zest, lemon juice, salt, pepper, and garlic in a food processor or blender. Pulse for 10–15 seconds, or until all of the ingredients are blended. Pour the ingredients into a small bowl. Add the parsley and the Stilton and blend into the sour cream mixture with a whisk. Cover and refrigerate for at least 4 hours before serving.

METHOD FOR THE SALAD

Rinse, drain, and tear all the salad greens into pieces. Place them in an 8-cup salad bowl. Toss in the scallions or garlic, celery, and mandarin oranges. Drizzle half the lemon cream dressing over the salad and toss lightly. Top the salad with the grape halves and cubes of Stilton. Drizzle with a little more dressing to taste and serve immediately.

VARIATION: *Use 1–2 fresh navel oranges (as in photo) or tart blood oranges instead of canned Mandarin orange sections. Peel the fresh oranges deep enough to remove all the white outside membrane, then make ¼-inch slices.*

PREP TIME: 20 minutes
YIELD: 7–8 cups salad
SERVES: 6–8

GORGONZOLA MASCARPONE TORTE

This blue-cheese torte, in all its variations a familiar sight at European tables for years, has only recently crossed the Atlantic. The pungent, creamy combination of mascarpone and Gorgonzola layers a sweeter dessert cheese with its tangy blue-veined cousin to produce a delicacy normally found only in specialty markets and restaurants.

PREP NOTES:

- *For a less rich torte, you may substitute homemade Stilton for the Gorgonzola.*

- *Plan for at least 8 hours' chilling time, or overnight. Before cutting the torte, allow it to rest at room temperature for about 5 minutes— it should remain firm and slice easily.*

SPECIAL EQUIPMENT

1-quart paté or metal mold

INGREDIENTS

16 ounces chilled Gorgonzola

8 ounces mascarpone, warmed to room temperature

1 teaspoon vegetable oil

2–4 ounces slightly chilled mascarpone for garnish

METHOD

Use a sharp stainless-steel knife to cut the Gorgonzola into slices ¼–⅜-inch thick. Place the slices on a dinner plate or flat serving dish and set aside until ready to use.

With a pastry brush, coat the bottom and sides of the mold with the vegetable oil. Gently press a slice of the Gorgonzola onto the bottom of the mold. Spoon the mascarpone onto the Gorgonzola, until the entire surface is covered with a layer approximately ¼ inch thick. Place a slice of the Gorgonzola on the mascarpone, and continue this process to create the layers of the torte.

Cover the mold with plastic wrap and chill for 8 hours in the refrigerator. Cover and refrigerate the remaining mascarpone for final assembly.

When ready to serve, take the torte from the refrigerator and remove the plastic wrap. Place the base and sides of the mold in a bowl of hot water for 2–3 minutes. Remove the mold and turn it onto a serving dish, open side down. Gently tap all sides with the handle of a butter knife and lift the mold pan from the cheese torte.

With a spatula or icing knife, spread the additional mascarpone over all sides of the torte. Serve with fruit and crackers.

PREP TIME: 20 minutes, plus 8 hours to chill
YIELD: 1½–pound torte
SERVES: 6–8

THREE-CHEESE HERB TORTE

Blend the right cheeses for a torte and you have a dish to delight guests' palates and please their eyes, both. This torte makes a substantial first course—plenty of flavor without too much body. The fresh ricotta remains firm, yet lighter than most commercial varieties.

SPECIAL EQUIPMENT

8-inch springform pan

INGREDIENTS

10 paper-thin slices fresh provolone cheese

6–8 large opal basil or mint leaves for garnish

Mild vegetable oil

RICOTTA MIXTURE INGREDIENTS

16 ounces fresh ricotta

½ cup Parmesan, freshly grated

¼ cup fresh parsley, minced

3 tablespoons fresh shallots, minced

2 tablespoons quality green extra-virgin olive oil

BASIL MIXTURE INGREDIENTS

½ cup fresh Genova or ordinary basil

½ cup fresh lemon basil

1 cup sun-dried tomatoes, minced

1 tablespoon fresh lemon zest

⅓ cup extra-virgin olive oil

PREP NOTE: *You can make the ricotta mixture a day ahead—just cover the bowl with plastic wrap and refrigerate.*

METHOD

Allow the ricotta to rest at room temperature for 15 minutes, or until pliable with a fork.

Using a pastry brush, coat the sides and the bottom of the springform pan with a light coating of mild vegetable oil and set the pan aside. In a medium glass bowl, blend the Parmesan, parsley, shallots, and olive oil with a wire whisk. Add the ricotta and continue to mix until all the ingredients are well blended.

Using a herb grinder or blender, mince the two basil varieties together and set aside. Combine the tomatoes, lemon zest, and olive oil in a small bowl and set aside.

Line the sides and bottom of the springform pan with 5 slices of the provolone. Spoon a third of the ricotta mixture on the bottom layer, followed by the minced basil. Spoon another third of the ricotta on top of the basil, followed by the tomatoes and lemon zest in olive oil. Top the tomatoes with the remaining ricotta.

To form the outer shell of the torte, place five slices of the provolone over the top of the torte, pressing to the edges of the pan. Cover with plastic wrap and refrigerate for at least 8 hours or overnight.

To serve, place the pan on a large plate or round serving platter. Release the sides of the pan. Garnish the torte with the mint or basil and serve with bread or toast.

PREP TIME: 20 minutes, plus 8 hours or overnight to chill

YIELD: 2½-pound torte

SERVES: 8–12

SWISS ONION FLATBREAD

This simple yet sturdy flatbread made from flour, leaven, water, and warm air, while distinctly Middle Eastern in origin, adapts itself to the palates of many cultures. I've experimented, with tasty results, by adding various seeds, spices and herbs, yogurt, and goat cheese to the dough, but the combination of Swiss cheese and onion remains a favorite. Serve this flatbread with soup, stews, as a first course with fruit, or as a pocket for your favorite sandwich.

INGREDIENTS

- 1 cup lukewarm water
- 1 package dry yeast
- 1 tablespoon sugar
- 3 cups bread flour, sifted
- 1 tablespoon salt
- 1½ cups Swiss cheese, shredded
- 3 tablespoons sesame seeds
- ½ cup grated yellow onion, drained
- 1 tablespoon vegetable oil

SERVING TIP: *Cut flatbread into pie-shaped wedges, then serve as a substitute for crackers with other appetizers.*

METHOD

In a medium bowl, gently blend the yeast and the water with a wire whisk. Add the sugar and stir once or twice to dissolve. Add the flour and the salt, mixing the ingredients with a fork, to form the dough. Add a little flour, if necessary, to avoid sticking. Knead the dough for 20–25 minutes, until it is smooth and satiny. Place the dough in a medium bowl. Cover the dough with plastic wrap, followed by a slightly damp towel. Set the bowl aside and allow the dough to rise in a warm, draft-free place for 1½ hours, or until it doubles in bulk.

Preheat the oven to 425°F. Punch the dough down. Add the Swiss cheese, sesame seeds, and onion, working the ingredients throughout the dough with your hands. Divide the dough into 6 equal parts and form each into a ball. With a rolling pin, roll each piece into a circle 4–5 inches across and ¼ inch thick.

Brush a baking sheet with the oil. Place the dough circles on the baking sheet and cover with a floured towel. Allow the dough to rise a second time, for another hour, until the circles double in size and become puffy.

Lift the dough circles and gently turn them over. Place them back onto the pan and bake for 15–20 minutes, or until golden and slightly crusty. Remove the bread from the oven and cover it with a towel for 20 minutes, or until cool.

Store in an airtight container or sealed freezer bag. This bread stays fresh for 2–3 days and keeps well in the freezer for up to 2 months.

PREP TIME: About 3 hours (including rising time)
YIELD: 6 flatbreads
SERVES: 6 modest eaters

LEMON MOZZARELLA WITH PARMESAN CROSTINI

This combination of mozzarella, lemon, olive oil, and fresh green olives comes alive with a side serving of Parmesan crostini, whose aroma while toasting may draw people to your kitchen from miles around. I serve this as finger food—toothpicks for the cheese, with crostini on the side.

PREP NOTE: *You can prepare crostini in advance—they will remain fresh in an airtight tin for up to 3 weeks. For knock-out flavor, however, prepare the mozzarella-olive mixture at room temperature and serve immediately.*

CROSTINI INGREDIENTS

- 1 slender French baguette
- ¾ cup quality extra-virgin olive oil
- 1 clove garlic, minced
- 1 tablespoon fresh rosemary, minced
- 2 tablespoons Parmesan, freshly grated
- ⅛ teaspoon cayenne or ½ teaspoon coarse-ground black pepper

METHOD

Preheat the oven to 350°F. Slice the bread into ⅜-inch rounds. Place the rounds on a baking sheet and set aside.

In a blender or food processor, combine the olive oil, rosemary, garlic, Parmesan, and cayenne. Pulse for 10–15 seconds. Pour into a small bowl. With a pastry brush, use half the olive oil-Parmesan mixture to coat one side of the bread slices.

Bake the bread on the middle rack of the oven for 5–7 minutes, or until lightly golden. Remove the baking sheet from the oven, turn the slices over, and brush with the remaining olive oil mixture. Bake another 5 minutes, remove from the oven, and set aside.

Allow the toasts to cool to room temperature. Serve immediately or store in an airtight container.

NOTE: *The crostini should be crisp on the outside, but a little chewy in the middle. If they are crisp through-out, they overstayed their welcome in the oven.*

LEMON MOZZARELLA INGREDIENTS

- 1 large clove fresh garlic
- 16 ounces fresh mozzarella in ½-inch cubes (or form homemade mozzarella into ½-inch balls)
- ¼ cup green picholine or small Spanish olives, drained
- ¼ cup Kalamata or other black imported olives, drained
- ¼ cup quality green extra-virgin olive oil
- Zest from 2 lemons
- ⅛ teaspoon green pepper-corns, freshly ground

METHOD

Rub the inside of a small wooden bowl with the garlic clove. Place the mozzarella and the olives in the bowl and gently toss with a slotted spoon. Add the olive oil and lemon zest. Toss again to blend the lemon zest throughout the mixture. Garnish with the green peppercorns, and serve with the Parmesan crostini.

PREP TIME: 30 minutes
YIELD: 2½–3 cups
SERVES: 4–6

FETA SPINACH OLIVE PIE

The creamy texture, firm body, and tang of Feta lend themselves to combinations with eggs, greens, cured ham, and grains. In this pie recipe, you can make both dough and filling in advance for worry-free assembly when you want to serve a few guests. Serve it with pita bread, grapes, and apples for a balanced, light meal.

main dishes & breads

PREP NOTE: *Bake this pie in a tart pan or a springform pan for the most elegant presentation.*

CRUST INGREDIENTS

- ¾ cup shortening
- ½ teaspoon salt
- ¼ cup boiling water
- 2½–3 cups sifted flour
- ⅓ cup cold milk

FILLING INGREDIENTS

- 4 jumbo eggs
- ½ cup whole milk
- 3 cups fresh spinach, chopped and drained, sprinkled with 1 tablespoon flour (to absorb some water while cooking)
- ½ cup scallions, chopped
- 2 tablespoon fresh parsley, chopped
- 2 cloves garlic, minced
- ¾ cup fresh Feta cheese, crumbled
- ¼ cup softened cream cheese
- ¼ teaspoon finely ground white pepper
- 3 ounces virgin olive oil or melted, unsalted butter
- ½ cup pitted Greek olives

METHOD

For the crust, in a medium mixing bowl, blend the shortening and water with a fork until the water is absorbed. Add the sifted flour and salt, and blend until the ingredients form a crumbly mass. Add the milk and blend until it is absorbed. Knead dough until smooth, cover with plastic wrap, and refrigerate until ready for final assembly.

Preheat the oven to 375°F. For the filling, in a large mixing bowl, stir the eggs with a wire whisk for 2–3 minutes, until blended. Add the milk, spinach, scallions, parsley, and garlic and blend together with a fork. Add the crumbled Feta, cream cheese, pepper, olive oil, and olives. With a slotted spoon, toss all the ingredients by hand for 2–3 minutes until evenly blended. Set the mixture aside.

Roll out the dough to ⅛-inch thickness and with it line the bottom and sides of a 9- to 10-inch springform pan. The dough will reach about halfway up the sides. Be sure to push the dough into the seam that connects the bottom to the sides, or the pie will separate when you release the form.

Pour the filling into the crust and bake for 30–40 minutes, or until the crust is golden and the top of the pie rises and remains slightly firm to the touch.

Remove the pie from the oven and allow it to rest in a warm spot for 10–12 minutes. Release the sides of the springform pan. Serve immediately.

PREP TIME: 1 hour and 15 minutes
SERVES: 6–8

GJETOST PIZZA

The unorthodox addition of creamy gjetost from Norway to the classic pizza pie only enhances it. Gjetost Pizza tastes especially good in the fall, when you can find peppers, onions, and herbs at the peak of flavor. Combine these with your homemade gjetost, and you may start getting phone calls from friends trying to order out. The recipe doubles reliably, if you decide to bake for a larger group of guests.

DOUGH INGREDIENTS

1¼ cups warm water

½ teaspoon sugar

1 package dry yeast

3½ cups bread flour

1 teaspoon salt

3 tablespoons butter, chipped

1 tablespoon quality extra-virgin olive oil

TOPPING INGREDIENTS

2 tablespoons extra-virgin olive oil

½ teaspoon black pepper, freshly ground

1 teaspoon garlic granules or powder

2 cups fresh mozzarella, shredded or thinly sliced

⅝ cup fresh gjetost, shredded

1 teaspoon white wine vinegar

1 teaspoon balsamic vinegar

3 orange or yellow bell peppers, roasted or grilled, then peeled, seeded, and chopped (instructions included here)

1½ cups fresh Walla Walla, Vidalia, or other sweet onion, chopped

2 tablespoons fresh parsley, chopped

½ teaspoon fine salt

2 tablespoons grated Parmesan

PREP NOTE: *You can make the dough up to 4–5 hours in advance of final prep. Cover it with plastic wrap and refrigerate it.*

METHOD FOR THE DOUGH

Pour the water into a small bowl. Add the sugar and whisk for 1–2 minutes until fairly well dissolved. Add the yeast and gently blend into the water mixture. Set aside in a warm, draft-free spot in the kitchen for 15 minutes, or until a layer of foam forms.

In a large glass bowl, combine the flour and salt with a fork or pastry blender. Add the butter and work it into the flour with your fingertips. Add the yeast mixture slowly, blending it into the flour until all of the liquid is completely absorbed. The dough should be moist but not sticky. Add a little more flour, if needed, for handling.

Turn the dough out onto a floured surface and knead it by hand for 15–20 minutes, or until the dough is elastic and silky in appearance. If you need to dust the dough with a little more flour to avoid sticking, do so sparingly. (Too much flour quickly overwhelms the elasticity, and the dough will become tough and somewhat tasteless.)

Pour the oil into a large bowl. Place the dough in the bowl and turn it in the oil until all sides of the dough are covered. Seal the bowl with plastic wrap and allow it to rest in a warm, draft-free spot for 45 minutes.

Preheat the oven to 375°F. Roll out the dough to a thickness of ¼–⅜ inches. Brush an 11x17 baking sheet with the olive oil. (The oil isn't necessary if you are using a baking stone.) Place the dough on the pan and push it to meet the edges on all sides, forming a lip to hold in the topping.

METHOD FOR THE ROASTED PEPPERS

To roast peppers, either scorch them over an open flame or roast them until well browned on a baking sheet in the oven at 500°F. Place the roasted peppers in a plastic or paper bag and seal the bag. Set aside for 20–30 minutes, allowing the peppers to cool down and pull away from their skins.

Remove the peppers from the bag and discard the charred skin, starting at the bottom of each pepper and working your way to the stem end. Once the pepper is clean, remove the stem and seeds with your hands and chop or set aside for future use. (Rinsing peppers of their seeds is a little less sticky than rubbing the seeds away with your fingers, but it also rinses off many of the chemical compounds that carry flavor.)

METHOD FOR THE TOPPING

Sprinkle the pepper and garlic onto the dough. Combine the vinegars, peppers, onions, parsley, and salt in a medium bowl.

Cover the dough with half the mozzarella. Add the pepper-onion mixture, followed by the gjetost. Top with the remaining mozzarella. Distribute the Parmesan over the entire pie.

Bake for 30–45 minutes, or until the pizza easily lifts away from the bottom of the pan and the cheeses are brown and bubbly. Serve immediately.

VARIATION: *The Gjetost-mozzarella combination marries well with tuna or crab meat.*

PREP TIME: 45–60 minutes for the dough; 1 hour for assembling and baking the pizza
YIELD: 11×17-inch pie
SERVES: 4–8

CHÈVRE DILL MUFFINS

Chèvre combines well with parsley, rosemary, and lemon thyme. Whether you roll this tangy goat cheese in herbs or simply keep it seasoned with a little salt and pepper, it complements almost any bread, year-round. Chèvre on toast is delectable, but chèvre baked into muffins is better. Try it with the dill called for in this recipe or experiment with your own favorite herbs.

INGREDIENTS

2 eggs, warmed to room temperature
1 cup whole milk
2 cups pastry flour, sifted
2 teaspoons baking powder
1 teaspoon baking soda
½ teaspoon salt
1 tablespoon sugar
⅛ teaspoon freshly ground white pepper
1 cup chèvre, well drained
2 tablespoons fresh chopped dill
¼ cup light vegetable oil

PREP NOTE: *This muffin batter adapts well for medium or large muffin pans.*

METHOD

Preheat the oven to 375°F. In a small bowl, lightly beat the eggs with a wire whisk. Stir the milk into the eggs until blended. Set the bowl aside.

Sift the dry ingredients together in a large mixing bowl. Stir in the egg-and-milk mixture just until the dry ingredients are moist. Gently blend the chèvre and dill into the muffin batter with a fork.

Brush the insides of a muffin tin with the vegetable oil. Spoon in the chèvre muffin batter so that each compartment is two-thirds full. Bake for 15–20 minutes, or until the muffins are firm and slightly golden. Remove the muffin pan from the oven and allow it to rest on a wire rack for 5–10 minutes, or until the muffins are cool enough to turn out of the pan. Serve warm.

PREP TIME: 30 minutes
YIELD: 12 medium or 6 large muffins

QUESO BLANCO ENCHILADAS
with Roasted Red Bell Sauce with Lime

Mexican food blends a wonderful complex of the earth's bounty. Chiles, tomatillos, herbs, cornmeal, and pintos congregate for innumerable partnerships of flavor and nutrition. However, they pale a bit without the creaminess and balance offered by homemade sour cream and table cheese. Baked or fried, queso blanco retains shape and body, a perfect filling for enchiladas.

SAUCE INGREDIENTS

- 4 red bell peppers, roasted, peeled, seeded, and chopped
- 4 roasted tomatillos, chopped
- 4 roasted plum tomatoes, chopped
- 3 tablespoons fresh cilantro, minced
- 2 tablespoons safflower oil
- 1 cup chopped sweet onion
- 2–3 fresh serrano chiles, seeded and chopped
- 1 teaspoon fresh coriander
- ½ teaspoon salt
- ¼ cup fresh lime juice
- 1 tablespoon fresh lime zest
- 1 cup table cream

NOTE: *Instructions for roasting peppers are included in the recipe for Gjetost Pizza on pages 122–23.*

FILLING INGREDIENTS

- 6 six-inch flour or white corn tortillas
- 2 tablespoons safflower oil
- 1 cup sweet onion, diced
- 1 cup fresh or canned medium-hot green chiles, roasted and diced
- 1–2 cloves garlic, peeled and minced
- 2½ cups queso blanco, in ¼- to ½-inch cubes
- 1 teaspoon ground cumin
- ⅛ teaspoon cinnamon
- ½ teaspoon salt
- 1½ cups homemade sour cream *(see box)*

PREP NOTE: *You can make both the sauce and the filling in this recipe a day or two before final assembly.*

METHOD

Place the roasted bell pepper, tomatillos, tomatoes, and cilantro in a food processor or blender and pulse for 3–5 seconds, until smooth yet slightly chunky. Set aside.

In a 2- or 3-quart saucepan, heat the oil, then add the onion and serrano chile. Sauté over medium-low heat for 10–15 minutes, or until the onion is slightly translucent. Add the pepper blend, fresh coriander, salt, lime juice, and zest, and cook for 30 minutes over low heat. Stir the sauce frequently to make sure that all the ingredients are well blended. Remove the pan from the heat and set aside.

For the filling, sauté the onions and garlic in a medium skillet over medium-low heat. *If using fresh chiles,* add them now and heat for 7–8 minutes, then add cumin and cinnamon; *if using canned chiles,* add them, the cumin, and cinnamon after heating for 7–8 minutes. Heat all ingredients for another 1–2 minutes.

HOMEMADE SOUR CREAM

Place 1 cup whipping cream and 3 tablespoons buttermilk in a 1-quart jar, screw the lid on tightly, and shake until well blended. Remove the lid and place the jar, uncovered, in a warm draft-free spot on your stove or near a pilot light, to thicken. Allow the mixture to stand for 8 hours or overnight, until it has the consistency of a milkshake. Put the lid back on the jar and transfer to the refrigerator. Chill for 6–8 hours before use.

Shelbyville-Shelby County Public Library

queso blanco enchiladas, cont.

Remove the pan from the heat and add the queso blanco and salt. Toss all the ingredients to blend the cheese and seasonings with the chiles and onion. Return the sauce to the stove, and heat until the mixture is lukewarm.

Preheat the oven to 375°F. For final assembly, spoon ¼–⅓ cup of the filling onto each tortilla. Roll the tortillas closed. Pour ¾ cup of the sauce into the bottom of a heavy baking dish. Place each stuffed tortilla into the dish, seam side down. With a pastry brush, coat the top of each tortilla with a little sauce. Bake for 20–25 minutes, or until the filling bubbles.

While the tortillas are baking, increase the heat under the saucepan so that the mixture is a little hotter than lukewarm. Add the table cream and blend into the sauce with a whisk. Cover the pot and reduce the heat to prevent scorching.

Remove the enchiladas from the oven. Spoon red bell pepper lime cream sauce over each. Garnish with homemade sour cream and serve hot.

PREP TIME: 45–60 minutes

YIELD: 6 enchiladas

HARVEST CHEDDAR POPPY BREAD

As you happily add your aged, handmade Cheddar to fruit, soups, eggs, and vegetables, remember that it also lends redolence and great flavor to bread, muffins, and desserts. Serve this Cheddar Poppy Bread with stews and hearty winter meals. You can make equally delicious bread from Cheddar made from either cow's or goat's milk. The recipe doubles reliably and keeps well in the freezer for up to 3 months.

INGREDIENTS

4 cups bread flour

1 package dry yeast

1 teaspoon sugar

½ teaspoon white pepper

1 teaspoon salt

1 cup lukewarm water

½ cup whole milk

1½ cups cow or goat Cheddar cheese, shredded

½ cup poppy seeds

1 egg white, lightly beaten with 1 tablespoon warm water

METHOD

Sift together the flour, yeast, sugar, pepper, and salt, then pour into a large bowl and set aside. In a small saucepan, combine the water and milk. Heat over medium heat for 10 minutes, or until the liquid reaches 110–120°F. Remove the pan from the stove and slowly stir the warm liquid into the dry ingredients. If necessary, stir in a little additional flour to form a soft but not sticky dough. Turn the dough out onto a floured surface and knead it for 15–20 minutes, or until elastic and satiny. Cover the dough with a towel and allow it to rest for 15 minutes.

Knead the Cheddar cheese into the dough. Add the poppy seeds a little at a time, working them into the dough until well blended. Place the dough in a greased 4½ x 8½-inch bread-loaf pan, where it needs to rise in a warm, draft-free spot in your kitchen for 1 hour or until doubled in size.

Preheat the oven to 375°F. Brush the loaf with the egg white mixture. Bake at 375°F for 30–40 minutes. The bread should be golden brown and sound slightly hollow when tapped. Remove the bread from the pan, turn the loaf on its side, and set it on a wire rack to cool. Serve, then wrap for the freezer.

PREP TIME: About 2½ hours

YIELD: 1 loaf

SERVES: 6–8

RAVIOLI TOSCANO

These Tuscany-inspired ravioli are delicious on two counts: handmade pasta, as well as handmade cheese. They make a lunch or dinner not only elegant but also a flavorful and nutritious. Try making and refrigerating the ravioli in the morning for serving later in the day. While stuffed pastas such as tortellini or ravioli may be made in larger batches and frozen, they taste best and retain a better texture created a few hours ahead of mealtime.

FILLING INGREDIENTS

2½ cups fresh ricotta

¾ cup Gorgonzola, cut
   into pieces

1 tablespoon fresh parsley

1 teaspoon fine white pepper

½ teaspoon lemon zest

1 egg yolk

SAUCE INGREDIENTS

½ cup rich chicken stock

¾ cup canned pumpkin,
   drained

½ teaspoon salt

½ teaspoon ground white
   pepper

1 cup whipping cream

1 tablespoon fresh chives,
   chopped

¼ cup toasted pumpkin seeds,
   hazelnut halves, or chopped
   fresh parsley (optional
   garnishes)

PASTA INGREDIENTS

4 jumbo eggs at room
   temperature

3–3¼ cups all-purpose
   unbleached flour

METHOD FOR THE FILLING

In a large mixing bowl, blend all the filling ingredients at low speed with a mixer for 2–3 minutes, until the mixture is somewhat smooth and well blended. Cover and refrigerate.

METHOD FOR THE SAUCE

In a blender or food processor, combine the chicken stock, pumpkin, salt, and pepper. Pulse for 1–2 minutes until the ingredients are smooth. Transfer to a 2-quart saucepan and cook over medium-low heat for 10–15 minutes until hot. Remove the pan from the heat and stir in the milk, followed by the cream and chives. Cover and set aside.

PREP NOTE: *If you want to make your pasta by hand and then roll the dough with a pasta machine, the instructions follow. If you plan to use a food processor, follow the instructions that accompany the equipment. The processing time by machine is shorter by 30 percent compared to processing by hand. Remember that overprocessing the dough will make it stiff and difficult to roll out.*

METHOD FOR THE PASTA

For hand-mixed pasta, form the flour into a mound on a kitchen countertop or other flat work surface. With your hand or a large spoon, push aside the flour from the middle of the mound, making a well for the eggs.

Place the eggs in the well and blend together with a fork. With the fork, pull flour from the sides of the well, blending and mixing with the beaten egg. Continue to work the flour into the egg mixture until it is completely absorbed. The dough should come together as a somewhat lumpy mass.

Begin to knead the dough with your hands, and add a little flour (a tablespoon or two at a time) if the dough becomes too sticky to handle. A certain amount of flour and small pieces of dough will stick to the work surface. Don't scrape them into the kneaded mass, because they make the dough lumpy, which defies the whole kneading process.

Continue to knead the dough for 15 minutes. It will be smooth, satiny, and very elastic in your hands. Wrap the dough in plastic wrap, or place it in a bowl covered tightly with plastic wrap. Allow the dough to relax for 30 minutes to 1 hour, to settle and breathe.

ASSEMBLY OF THE RAVIOLI

For final assembly, remove the ricotta-Gorgonzola filling from the refrigerator and set aside.

Cut the dough in halves or quarters, according to your preference. Using either a rolling pin or pasta machine, roll the dough several times until it is stretched to $\frac{1}{16}$ to $\frac{1}{8}$ inch thick. Thinner pasta dough requires less cooking time and is less apt to be chewy or tough.

Roll the dough to even thickness, in sheets about 4–5 inches wide. Spoon rounded teaspoonsful of the filling along one long side of the dough, 2–3 inches apart. Fold the dough lengthwise to create a long tube. Use a fork or fluted pastry wheel to join the edges and ends of each tube, completely sealing all sides. Use a knife or pastry cutter to cut across the tubes, in between the mounds of filling inside. You now have a row of ravioli squares. Transfer these to a dry towel. Continue this process until you have used all of the dough and filling.

The ravioli are ready to cook immediately. However, if you plan to cook them a few hours after making, be sure to turn them from side to side so that they dry evenly. Avoid layering them or allowing the ravioli to touch each other, because they will stick together.

FINAL TOUCHES AND COOKING

Preheat the oven to "Warm," and warm an oven-proof platter for serving the ravioli.

Return the pumpkin cream sauce to the stove and allow it to sit over very low heat—hot, but not bubbling—for about 15 minutes, to thicken.

In a large (4-quart) soup pot or Dutch oven, bring 2–3 quarts of water to a boil. Add one table-spoon of salt, and drop the ravioli in. They will fall to the bottom of the pot, then slowly rise to the surface as they cook. Simmer the ravioli for 5–10 minutes until the pasta floats on the surface. Remove one ravioli from the pot and test it for tenderness. If the dough tastes or feels under-cooked, allow the pasta to simmer for 1–2 minutes longer.

Lift the ravioli from the pot with a slotted spoon and allow them to drain for a moment before transferring to the heated serving dish. Ladle the warm pumpkin cream sauce over the ravioli and garnish with fresh chopped parsley, if you wish. Serve hot.

PREP TIME: Take the afternoon off to make ravioli

YIELD: About 16 ounces of pasta

SERVES: 4–6

desserts

RICOTTA PIE

Fresh ricotta transforms ordinary cheesecake into a lighter fare, which you may choose to serve as a side dish with salads, eggs, and fruit, as well as for dessert. The recipe here is generous enough to set a large group of guests moaning with pleasure. You can make it ahead, it refrigerates well, and you can assemble it as much as 24 hours before you present it on your table.

PREP NOTE: *Pie must be refrigerated for 8 hours before serving.*

SPECIAL EQUIPMENT

9- to 10-inch springform pan

CRUST INGREDIENTS

2½ cups all-purpose flour, sifted

1 teaspoon double-acting baking powder

¼ teaspoon salt

¼ cup granulated sugar

½ cup unsalted butter

2 eggs, slightly beaten

¼ cup whole milk

¼ teaspoon vanilla

FILLING INGREDIENTS

5 eggs

1½ cups granulated sugar

½ teaspoon salt

2 pounds fresh ricotta

1 teaspoon vanilla

1 teaspoon fresh lemon zest

½ teaspoon fresh lemon juice

METHOD

Preheat oven to 350°F. For the crust, in a medium mixing bowl, sift together the flour, baking powder, salt, and sugar. Using a fork or pastry cutter, blend in the butter until the mixture is crumbly. Add the eggs, milk, and vanilla and blend into the flour. Work all the ingredients into a smooth ball. Roll out onto lightly floured waxed paper until ⅛ inch thick. Transfer the dough to the springform pan and refrigerate while you make the filling.

For the filling, in a large mixing bowl, use a mixer to blend the egg with the sugar and salt. Add the ricotta, vanilla, lemon zest, and lemon juice. Mix all the ingredients until smooth and well blended. Remove the springform pan from the refrigerator. Ladle the filling into the pan and bake for 60–70 minutes, until the pie is firm around the perimeter while moist and pliant in the middle, and the crust is golden. Gently remove from the oven and transfer to a draft-free area of your kitchen.

Allow the pie to cool completely and refrigerate for 8 hours before serving.

PREP TIME: About 1½ hours, and 8 hours for chilling

SERVES: 12

A PERSONAL NOTE: *This pie has been an Easter tradition in our family for three generations. I grew up watching my mom perfect the crust and the filling from my grandmother's handwritten notes. This is her recipe.*

TIRAMISU TANGO

The Venetian who developed tiramisu must have needed a pick-me-up, because that is the literal translation of this Italian dessert, a rich mix of espresso, sugar, and egg yolks. Ease of assembly and serving versatility only add to its perfection—you can create individual servings or arrange all of the ingredients in one large dish. If the combination of eggs and sugar gives tiramisu its body, your homemade mascarpone gives it soul.

PREP NOTES:

- *It's best to make the mascarpone cream and allow it to refrigerate for 1 hour before final assembly. (In dire straits, you may substitute 3 cups whipped heavy cream for the cheese.)*

- *This dessert refrigerates well and can be assembled 2 hours in advance of serving.*

RAW EGG ALERT

When you are serving uncooked eggs, as in this recipe:

- **Know your source— use only good-quality fresh eggs.**

- **Do not serve them to the very young, the very old, or the immunosuppressed.**

INGREDIENTS

      6   large egg yolks
    ¼   cup finely granulated sugar
      3   cups mascarpone
      2   tablespoons hazelnut brandy
          or coffee
    36   ladyfingers
   3–4   cups espresso or strong coffee,
          slightly chilled
    ½   cup dark chocolate, shaved
          and blended with ½ teaspoon
          ground cinnamon

METHOD

To make the mascarpone cream, in a
medium mixing bowl, blend the egg
yolks and sugar together with a mixer
until creamy and lemony in color.
Add the mascarpone and the brandy.
Mix until all ingredients are blended
and fluffy. Cover the bowl and refrigerate for 1 hour.

For assembly, remove the mascarpone from the refrigerator and set
aside. Arrange half of the ladyfingers
on a shallow serving platter. Slowly
drizzle with half of the espresso or
coffee until covered and moist. With
spatula, spread half of the mascarpone cream on top of the ladyfingers.
Add another layer of ladyfingers,
drizzling them with the remaining
cold espresso. Top with the second
half of the mascarpone cream.
Garnish with the shaved chocolate
and serve immediately or refrigerate
until needed.

PREP TIME: About 20 minutes
      to assemble, 1 hour to chill
SERVES: 8–12

FROMAGE STRAWBERRY WREATH

Fromage blanc speaks for itself. One of the most digestible of
cheeses, it complements fresh berries, peaches, or steamed
vegetables with equal ease. If you're experimenting, it also
combines well with yogurt and other cheeses—cottage or
cream cheese or (as in this recipe) ricotta. For a light, sumptu-
ous dessert, add a taste of orange and cinnamon to the
cheese and serve with your favorite summer fruits. (See the
photo, page 36.)

INGREDIENTS

⅝ cup fresh fromage blanc	2 tablespoons fresh-squeezed orange juice
⅝ cup fresh ricotta	12–16 large, fresh strawberries
⅛ teaspoon cinnamon	4–6 sprigs fresh orange, lemon, or lime mint or lemon verbena (for garnish)
¼ teaspoon fresh orange zest	

PREP NOTE: *This recipe doubles easily
and may be prepared in advance*

METHOD

Place the fromage blanc and ricotta in a small mixing bowl
and stir with a wire whisk until creamy and fairly smooth.
Add the cinnamon, orange zest, and orange juice. Stir until
these ingredients are blended into the cheese mixture.

Mound the fromage blanc–ricotta mixture in the center of
a flat serving dish. Arrange the fresh strawberries to form a
wreath around the cheese. Garnish with fresh orange mint
and serve chilled.

SERVING TIP: *For a more exotic and decadent dessert, melt
4 ounces of white chocolate in a small double boiler, along with
2 tablespoons of raspberry (frambois) liqueur. Drizzle the
strawberries with the warm raspberry chocolate before serving.*

PREP TIME: 20 minutes
SERVES: 4–6

GOUDA APPLE COBBLER

Who is there with taste buds so dead that they don't salivate over a warm cobbler? The chopped pecans and homemade Gouda in this recipe raise the humble cobbler to new heights. Here, a Gouda that has aged a while adds honeyed sweetness to the apple filling. Savor this dessert on its own or add ice cream, if you must. Serve it for breakfast, lunch, midafternoon treats, dinner, bedtime snacks...

CRUST INGREDIENTS

- 2 cups unbleached white flour, sifted
- 3 teaspoons baking powder
- ¼ teaspoon salt
- 2 tablespoons refined sugar
- ¼ teaspoon allspice
- ¼ cup butter
- ½ cup milk

FILLING INGREDIENTS

- 3 cups ripe yellow-delicious apples, sliced
- 3 cups red baking apples, sliced
- ½ cup golden baking raisins
- ½ cup pecans, chopped
- ⅔ cup white sugar
- ⅓ cup light brown sugar, tightly packed
- 1 cup Gouda, shredded
- 1 tablespoon lemon juice
- 3 tablespoons flour
- ¼ teaspoon ground nutmeg
- ¼ teaspoon ground cinnamon

METHOD

For the crust, sift together the flour, baking powder, salt, sugar, and allspice and transfer to a mixing bowl. Add the butter and milk (increase or decrease the milk according to the crust texture you prefer) and blend all the ingredients with a fork until they form a crumbly mixture. Set aside.

Preheat the oven to 375°F. Butter a 2-quart oblong baking dish and set aside.

Toss the apples with the raisins, pecans, sugars, and Gouda. Add the lemon juice, flour, nutmeg, and cinnamon, and continue to toss all of the ingredients until blended. Transfer the Gouda-apple mixture to the baking dish. Spoon the flour mixture over the fruit and bake for 30–40 minutes or until golden. Serve warm.

PREP TIME: 1¼ hours to make and bake
SERVES: 8–10

cheese-makers'
sources for Equipment, Supplies, and Information

AMERICAN CHEESE SOCIETY

W 7702 County Road
Darien, WI 53114
USA

PHONE 414.728.4458

FAX 414.728.1658

WEBSITE www.cheesesociety.org

Members are interested in the production of farmhouse and handcrafted cheeses and American cheese making. Newsletter, tips on making cheese, member directory.

ASTELL SCIENTIFIC (U.K.)

PHONE 011.44.181.300.4311
Starter cultures and molds.

CAPRINE SUPPLY

33001 West 83rd
Desoto, KS 66018
USA

PHONE 913.585.1191

Dairy goat supplies, starter cultures, molds, presses, other cheese-making equipment.

Free catalog.

CUMBERLAND GENERAL STORE

Route 3, Box 81
Crossville, TN 38855
USA

PHONE 931.484.8481

A wide variety of hardware and cheese-making supplies. Catalog for $4.00, information about cheese making free.

GLENGARRY CHEESEMAKING AND DAIRY SUPPLIES

RR #2
Alexandria, ON K0C 1A0
Canada

PHONE 613.525.3133

FAX 613.525.3394

WEBSITE www.cheese.com

A complete range of cultures, supplies, and equipment for most varieties of homemade soft and hard cheese. Website offers a catalog and information about seminars, books, and videos.

HOEGGER SUPPLY COMPANY

160 Providence Road
Fayetteville, GA 28303
USA

PHONE 770.461.4129

Complete line of goat and cheese-making supplies.

Free catalog.

LEHMAN HARDWARE AND APPLIANCES

LOCATION 1 Lehman Circle
MAILING ADDRESS P.O. Box 41
Kidron, OH 44636
USA

PHONE 330.857.5757

FAX 330.857.5785

EMAIL Getlehmans@aol.com

WEBSITE www.lehmans.com

A full range of cheese-making starters, kits, equipment, and presses. Catalog for $3.00, or available on the Internet.

NATIONAL DAIRY COUNCIL

5–7 John Princes Street
London W1M 0AP
UK

PHONE 011.44.171.499.7822

Entertaining and fairly substantial information about British cheese, its history, production, and nutrition. Invaluable source of informaiton about a number of dairies and equipment suppliers.

NEW ENGLAND CHEESEMAKING SUPPLY

85 Main Street
Ashfield, MA 01330
USA

PHONE 413.628.3808

EMAIL info@cheesemaking.com

WEBSITE www.cheesemaking.com

Starter cultures, wax, cheesecloth, equipment, molds, presses, and literature about making cheese. Catalog for $1.00; a copy comes with every mail order shipment. Call for information or consult their website.

P. TEXEL LTD. (U.K.)

PHONE 011.44.161.910.1500
pH meters and other equipment

WISBY CORPORATION

Starter Cultures and Media

4215 N. Port Washington Road
Milwaukee, WI 53212
USA

PHONE 414.332.4790

FAX 414.332.7206

Specialists available for problem solving; helpful printed information about media and cultures.

metric equivalents

DRY WEIGHTS

U.S.	Metric
½ ounce	10 grams
1 ounce	14 grams
2 ounces	57 grams
4 ounces (¼ pound)	114 grams
8 ounces (½ pound)	227 grams
16 ounces (1 pound)	464 grams

LIQUID WEIGHTS

U.S.	Metric
1 teaspoon	5 ml
1 tablespoon (3 teaspoons)	15 ml
2 tablespoons (1 ounce)	30 ml
¼ cup	60 ml
⅓ cup	80 ml
1 cup (8 ounces)	240 ml
2 cups (1 pint)	480 ml
4 cups (1 quart)	1 liter
4 quarts (1 gallon)	3.75 liters

LENGTH

U.S.	Metric
1 inch	2.5 cm

OVEN TEMPERATURES

U.S.	Metric
32°F (water freezes)	0°C
212°F	100°C
300°F (slow oven)	150°C
350°F (moderate oven)	175°C
400°F (hot oven)	205°C

To convert Fahrenheit to Celsius:

subtract 32, multiply by 5, and divide by 9

Photograph courtesy of WISCONSIN MILK MARKETING BOARD.

glossary

ACID CURD The curd that results from milk high in acidity. When warmed milk is inoculated with starter-culture bacteria, the milk sugar (lactose) undergoes a chemical change that produces acid.

AGING Storing pressed or molded cheese at a specific temperature and humidity to develop a certain flavor

ALBUMINOUS PROTEIN A milk protein that forms a deposit (such as ricotta curd) as a result of the application of direct heat instead of rennet, which cannot force albuminous protein out of milk

ANNATTO A yellowish-red dye extracted from the seed pulp of the Caribbean annoto tree. One or two drops added to cheese curds results in a pale- to orangish-yellow cheese.

BACTERIAL LINENS Rod-shaped bacteria that produce the outer reddish-brown mold smear used to ripen such cheeses as Muenster and brick. Blended with water in an atomizer, the linens are sprayed directly onto the surface of the cheese during the aging process, creating a linenlike effect as the mold grows.

BAG CHEESE Any cheese (Feta, queso blanco, Muenster) that gains shape as a solid mass by hanging to drain in a cheesecloth sack or bag.

BANDAGING Binding or pressing cheese with a coarse cheesecloth or other mesh cloth to encourage a desired shape

BLOOMY RIND The kind of thin, white, smooth rind that forms as a semisoft cheese such as Brie or Camembert ripens, after the cheese is sprayed with mold spores to promote ripening from the outside in. The delicate powdery coating is called a *bloom*.

BLUE-VEINED CHEESE Any cheese, such as Stilton, Danish blue, or Gorgonzola, that forms veins or striations of blue mold throughout the cheese during the ripening process. The mold is the result of either dusting or inoculating with Roquefort penicillin.

BUTTERCLOTH Finely woven cloth used to drain whey off butter and cheese

CAPILASE The enzyme that produces the sharp flavor in such Italian cheeses as provolone or Romano

CASEIN The protein "backbone" of cheese that reacts to heat and rennet to form curds and expel whey until the curds condense into a mass

CHEDDARING Cutting condensed curds into strips and allowing them to set in warm conditions, in preparation for salting and pressing

CHEESE COLOR A liquid dye called annatto that lends a golden or orange color to cheese

CHEESE MAT A woven, fairly porous reed mat used in draining the whey from soft cheeses and air drying harder cheeses, and as a "saucer" under cheeses aging in a cool room or refrigerator

CHEESE PRESS A mechanical device involving a mold, a draining tray, and pressure that binds, shapes, and drains cheese curds

CHEESE WRAP A clear cellophane-like sheet of plastic that helps maintain proper air flow and humidity when used to wrap bloomy- mold and soft cheese for aging and storing

CHEESECLOTH Woven cotton cloth that acts as a sieve, used to drain whey from cheese

CITRIC ACID Typically extracted from lemons, a substance that can encourage the breakdown of lactose into the lactic acid necessary to the formation and suspension of curds

CLEAN CUT or BREAK The clean knife separation of curds that have been infused with rennet and allowed to set

CURD The thick substance that results when protein and fat are extracted from milk, through the infusion of rennet or citric acid

CUTTING CURD Reducing the curd to pieces of equal size with a long-blade sterile knife

DAIRY THERMOMETER A device that can either float or attach to the side of a double boiler to measure the temperature of milk (0–212°F)

DRIP TRAY A shallow tray usually placed under a cheese mold to collect drained-off whey

ENZYMES Living cells of protein that cause biochemical reactions at certain temperatures

FLAKE SALT Coarse, noniodized salt

FLORA DANICA A bacteria culture used in the making of various types of goat cheese, including Camembert

FLOWER The scent or aroma of cheese, especially bloomy cheeses such as Brie

FOLLOWER A block of material, usually wood, that helps supply pressure and balance in the cheese-press mold by filling any gap between the pound gauge and the curds

FOOT A French colloquial expression referring to the bottom and sometimes the side walls of a bloomy cheese such as Brie. The foot can retain a somewhat bitter flavor, and some cheese lovers caution that "you never cut into the foot."

FOREWORKING Stirring fresh-cut curds to keep them separated

FROMAGE A fresh white, smooth goat cheese, often served for dessert or as a substitute for cream cheese or mascarpone

HOMOGENIZATION In milk, the mechanical process that blends the fat with the other components, so that it no longer separates or rises to the top

HYGROMETER An instrument that measures the humidity of the atmosphere

INOCULATION Introducing pathogens into milk to stimulate the production of bacteria

LACTIC ACID The acid that results from the breakdown of lactose (milk sugar) infused with rennet or citric acid

LACTOSE The sugar found in milk

LIPASE POWDER An enzyme that encourages a chemical process that results in flavor, frequently used to encourage and enhance the flavor of Italian cheeses such as Parmesan

MESOPHILIC STARTER CULTURE A bacterial culture that triggers enzymatic activity for cheeses that require lower, or warm, temperatures to form curds

MILLING Heating and breaking hot curds into smaller pieces

MOLD-RIPENED CHEESE Cheese that receives its identifying flavor and texture through the growth of mold on its surface, its interior, or, in some cases, both

NATURAL RIND The outer rind that a cheese develops while air drying and aging

NEEDLING Piercing a cheese with a long instrument (such as an ice pick). Blue-veined cheeses frequently get pierced from one side to the other, so that the applied bacteria can trigger mold growth throughout.

PASTEURIZATION Destroying unwanted bacteria by heating milk to 144–145°F and keeping it at that temperature for 30 minutes

PASTY The dry, sometimes chalky texture of cheese that has been overdrained

PENICILLIUM CANDIDUM Bacteria used to cover the outer surface of semisoft cheese such as Camembert in order to grow the mold that makes the bloomy white rind

pH BALANCE The ratio of acid to alkaline

PRESSING The draining off of whey and molding of a cheese into a desired shape

PROPRIONIC CULTURE The bacterial culture that causes the gases to form that make pressed curds swell up and stretch, causing the "eyes" that appear in cheeses such as Swiss or Emmenthaler

RAW MILK Fresh milk that has not been pasteurized

glossary, *continued*

RED BACTERIA Also known as bacterial linens, or a smear, these are applied to the outer surface of some cheeses, such as brick or Muenster, to encourage mold growth that improves flavor and texture.

RENNET A powder or liquid that contains rennin, the enzyme that forces coagulation in warm, cultured milk

RIPENING The development of acidity as a result of the infusion of a cheese starter-culture bacteria

SALTING Adding noniodized flake salt to loose curds or to the surface of pressed cheeses to encourage drying and help ward off possible contamination

SEEDING Adding fungus or bacteria to curds to encourage the growth of mold that assists aging. For instance, blue-veined cheeses are seeded with *Penicillium candidum*, which promotes the development of blue-mold spores.

SEMISOFT CHEESE Any cheese that has been drained and molded, but not pressed, to form its body and outer rind. With a high moisture content, semisoft cheeses usually age for a relatively short time.

SOFT CHEESE Molded cheese that has been drained, yet maintains a high moisture content. Soft cheese can be eaten fresh or aged briefly.

SOUL A soft ripened cheese molded into a thick shape that prevents even ripening, so the cheese develops a thick, somewhat chalky "soul," or center, and remains runny near the crust. Such a cheese is not only edible but delicious.

STARTER CULTURE The bacterial culture that initiates the development of curds in warmed milk

STIRRING CURD Turning, or stirring, curds to expel whey

SURFACE CULTURES Bacterial cultures sprayed onto the outer surface of cheese to encourage the growth of mold during aging

TARTARIC ACID A plant compound usually present in fragrant, acidic liquids such as vinegar

THERMOPHILIC STARTER CULTURE A sturdy bacterial culture that encourages reactivity in milk heated to higher temperatures

TOP STIRRING Stirring the top ¼ inch of milk to prevent cream from rising after the addition of rennet

ULTRAPASTEURIZED MILK Milk pasteurized long enough at high temperatures to contain no significant bacteria life. This milk will not produce cheese.

WAX A colored paraffin, usually red, black, or yellow, used to cover and protect aging cheese and to stabilize its moisture balance

WHEY The liquid that remains after milk proteins coagulate, containing water, sugar, albuminous protein, and minerals but no fat

WHITE MOLD The mold that develops when a cheese surface has been sprayed with bacteria that cause spore growth. Also known as *Penicillium candidum*, it is characteristic of Brie, Camembert, and other bloomy soft cheeses.

bibliography

Beck, Simone. *Simca's Cuisine*. New York: Knopf, 1972.

Brennan, Ethel, and Brennan, Georgeanne. *Goat Cheese*. San Francisco: Chronicle, 1997.

Carroll, Ricki, and Carroll, Robert. *Cheesemaking Made Easy*. Vermont: Storey, 1996.

Casas, Penelope. *Delicioso! The Regional Cooking of Spain*. New York: Knopf, 1996.

Chelminsky, Rudolph. "Ooh la la!" *Smithsonian*, December 1996.

Chesser, Jerald W. *The Art and Science of Culinary Preparation*. American Culinary Federation, 1992.

Dunne, Lavon J. *Nutrition Almanac*. New York: McGraw-Hill, 1990.

Hazan, Marcella. *Essentials of Classic Italian Cooking*. New York: Knopf, 1992.

Jenkins, Steve. *Cheese Primer*. New York: Workman, 1996.

Kasper, Lynne. *The Splendid Table*. New York: Morrow, 1992.

La Place. *Cucina Fresca*. New York: Harper & Row, 1995.

Loomis, Susan Herrmann. *French Farmhouse Cookbook*. New York: Workman, 1996.

Mont-Laurier Benedictine Nuns. *Goat Cheese: Small Scale Production*. Ashfield, Mass.: New England Cheesemaking Supply Company, 1983.

Nanet, Bernard. *Cheeses of the World*. New York: Rizzoli, 1993.

Parsons, Russ. *A Cheesemaker's Buffalo Dreams*. Los Angeles Times, home edition, March 18, 1998.

Paston-Williams, Sara. *The Art of Dining*. Oxford: National Trust Enterprises,1993.

Root, Waverly. *Food*. New York: Konecky and Konecky, 1980.

Trager, James. *Food Chronology*. New York. Holt, 1995.

Turgeon, Charlotte, ed. *The Creative Cooking Course*. New York: Weathervane, 1982.

Weisby Corporation. *Weisby Product Guide*. Neibull, Ger.: Weisby, 1997.

Photograph courtesy of National Park Service Carl Sandburg Home National Historic Site.

Hooked on Cheese Making

You never know where a little kitchen cheese making may take you. Look at Jane North, for example. At the Northland Sheep Dairy in Marathon, New York, she and her husband, Karl, today specialize in creating organic cheese from sheep's milk. They also make Tomme beergere, fashioned after the Spanish Manchego, and Bergere bleue, which has won national acclaim. And it all started at home.

Jane North traces her fascination with the properties of milk to her childhood. "It was my mother, who was not a farmer, who first demonstrated for me the magical transformation of milk from liquid to standstill solid. For special treats, especially when we children were confined to our beds with some minor illness, she made Junket by using those little tablets called rennet and allowed us to choose the drop of color to be added. It always made us feel so much better if the junket was blue or pale pink."

In the late 1960s, Jane North's serious affair with cheese began: "The preservation of milk as cheese—putting it by for the winter—presented itself to me naturally, as part of the harvest season when my own family became caretakers of our friend's farm during her vacation. Sometime between freezing the peas and canning the tomatoes, the need arose to 'do something' with the extra goat milk. So began numerous trials of ripening pressed cheeses. I was hooked."

Since then, North has farmed in the Eastern Pyrenees of France, walked through the caves in Roquefort, and seriously studied the manufacture of blue-veined cheese. She began producing cheese for market in 1988.

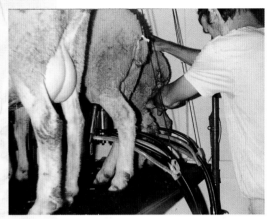

"I still love the idea of preserving milk for another day," Jane North says, "and the fact that virtually anyone with access to good clean milk can make cheese at home in the kitchen."
Photograph of Karl North
courtesy of Northland Dairy.

index

acidification, 20
American Cheese Society, 23, 136
Amish, 16

blue, Danish, 74–76;
    Danish Sesame Twists, 110
Bread, Harvest Cheddar Poppy, 126
brick, all-American, 71–73

Camembert, 77–79;
    Camembert Phyllo, 111
Caprine Supply, 136
Cheddar: Harvest Cheddar Poppy Bread, 126;
    sage, 90;
    white goat, 84–86;
    yellow aged, 87–89
cheese presses, 31, 67
chèvre, 38–39;
    Chèvre Dill Muffins, 123
Ciccione, Virgilio and Jerry, 61
Cobbler, Gouda Apple, 134–35
cottage cheese, 49–51
cream cheese, 47–48
Crostini, Lemon Mozzarella with Parmesan, 118–19
Cumberland General Store, 136
curds, 20–22

Danish Sesame Twists, 110

Egg Farm Dairy, 12
Enchiladas, Queso Blanco, 125–26
equipment, 24–25, 136

Fafatch, Polly, 35
fermentation, 20

Feta, 82–83;
    Feta Spinach Olive Pie, 120–21
Flatbread, Swiss Onion, 117
Fondue, Serenely Swiss, 108–9
fromage blanc, 36–37;
    Fromage Blanc Strawberry Wreath, 36, 133

Gjetost, 106–7;
    Gjetost Pizza, 122–23
Gouda, Holland, 91–93;
    Gouda Apple Cobbler, 134–35

herb garden cheese, 42–44
Hoegger Supply Company, 136

Il Forteto, 13
Italcheese, 61

Lakehaven Farms, 35
Lehman Hardware and Appliances, 136
Leipäjuusto, Finnish, 35, 45–46

mascarpone, 40–41;
    Gorgonzola Mascarpone Torte, 114;
    Tiramisu Tango, 132–33
Mildbrand, Jim, 76
milk, 26–27;
    pasteurizing, 26; tips on, 35
mozzarella, 57–59;
    braided, 62–63;
    smoked, 64;
    stuffed, 60;
    Lemon Mozzarella with Parmesan Crostini, 118–19
Mozzarella Company, 34
mozzarella di buffala, 61

Muenster, 80–81
Muffins, Chèvre Dill, 123

New England Cheesemaking Supply, 136
North, Jane, 142
Northland Sheep Dairy, 142
Parmesan, 15, 97–99;
    Lemon Mozzarella with Parmesan Crostini, 118–19;
    Three-Cheese Herb Torte, 116

Phyllo, Camembert, 111
Pie, Feta Spinach Olive, 120–21;
    Ricotta, 130–31
Pizza, Gjetost, 122–23

queso blanco, 52-53;
    Queso Blanco Enchiladas, 125–26

raclette, 100–102
Ravioli Tuscano, 127-29
Rennet, 20
ricotta: Ravioli Tuscano, 127–29;
    Ricotta Pie, 130–31;
    Three-Cheese Herb Torte, 116;
    whole- cream, 54–55;
    whey, 56;
Romano, 94–96

Salad, Stilton Spring, 112–13
Sandburg, Helga, 8
Sarti, Stephano, 13
scamorze, 64
starter culture, 20, 28–29;
    making your own, 29

Stilton, 68–70;
    Stilton Spring Salad, 112–13
supplies, 25, 136
Swiss, baby, 103–5;
    Serenely Swiss Fondue, 109;
    Swiss Onion Flatbread, 117

Tiramisu Tango, 132–33
Torte, Gorgonzola Mascarpone, 114–15;
    Three-Cheese Herb, 116

weinkase, 65–67
whey, 20–22; collecting, 21
White, Jonathan, 12
Williams, Jesse, 17
Wisby Corporation, 76, 136
Wisconsin Cheese Makers Association, 19